THE WALK OF THE CROSS

THE WALK OF THE CROSS

Christian Discipleship: Dying to Self

Robert H. Makrush

ELM HILL

A Division of
HarperCollins Christian Publishing

www.elmhillbooks.com

The Walk of the Cross
Christian Discipleship: Dying to Self

Published in Nashville, Tennessee, by Elm Hill, an imprint of Thomas Nelson. Elm Hill and Thomas Nelson are registered trademarks of HarperCollins Christian Publishing, Inc.

Elm Hill titles may be purchased in bulk for educational, business, fund-raising, or sales promotional use. For information, please e-mail SpecialMarkets@ ThomasNelson.com.

All Scripture quotations are taken from the Holy Bible, New International Version', NIV'. Copyright © 1973, 1978, 1984, 2011 by Biblica, Inc.' Used by permission of Zondervan. All rights reserved worldwide. www.Zondervan.com. The "NIV" and "New International Version" are trademarks registered in the United States Patent and Trademark Office by Biblica, Inc.'

Library of Congress Cataloging-in-Publication Data

Library of Congress Control Number: 2019914875

ISBN 978-1-400328987 (Paperback)
ISBN 978-1-400328994 (Hardbound)
ISBN 978-1-400329007 (eBook)

TABLE OF CONTENTS

THE WALK OF THE CROSS
CHRISTIAN DISCIPLESHIP: DYING TO SELF

Throughout the ages, the majority of Christians have referred to themselves as members of a church rather than disciples, believing disciples were only the original twelve whom Jesus called to follow Him during His earthly ministry. Yet, the word "disciple" in Greek literally means a "learner." It captures the idea of a disciple as being one who attaches himself to a teacher and follows his teaching. Thus a disciple of Jesus is one who is following and learning from Jesus through the revelation of Scripture. As Christians, we also tend to ignore the fact that Jesus' Great Commission to make disciples is predicated on first, being a disciple and second, that discipleship is a lifelong process with a cost—dying to self. It begins with faith in Christ and continues with an evergrowing cost of commitment to develop an intimate spiritual personal relationship with the Lord through belief in Scripture.

Christians have traditionally used the forty days prior to Easter, known as Lent, as a time to rededicate ourselves to the imitation of

Christ. Some of us abstain from pleasurable things like chocolate or TV in an attempt to purify ourselves from worldly desires. Others prefer to add some additional religious aspect to our lives like a Lenten devotional, additional prayer time, or some worthy church social function. Whether we abstain or add, there is a conscious effort to revive our Christian discipleship by identifying with Christ's teaching and journey of passion for our salvation. Doing these activities in small groups makes this also a time to renew fellowship within church.

"The Walk of the Cross" is a Lenten study designed to help Christians search their hearts and souls as well as rededicate themselves to be faithful Disciples of Christ. It is a daily devotional which examines fundamental biblical beliefs in context with several scriptures each day. Daily readings are followed by questions for reflection and journaling. Jesus used this method of rabbinic teaching when he asked questions of His disciples such as "Who do you say (believe) I am?", "Why do you call me good?", or "To what shall I compare the Kingdom of God?" Journaling, scripture reading, and Spirit-led prayers form the foundation of this personal study as we consider what we really should believe concerning issues such as God's calling, grace, salvation, sanctification, and regeneration. The process allows the Holy Spirit to confront false beliefs as well as alleviate areas of doubt in our faith.

As for those who may be asking what difference it makes how one believes, professionals have long known that our beliefs, especially those concerning morals, ethics, and religion, control how we think, feel, and behave. Our beliefs do this by coming together to form attitudes and prejudices concerning who we are and the world around us. Because our belief systems work with a high degree of automation, they can be easily influenced and even corrupted by the culture of the world. Therefore, we should always actively consider what and how we believe under the guidance of the Spirit. Consider the fact that the Gospels detail how Jesus spent the better part of three years training and correcting the beliefs, attitudes, and prejudices of His disciples. Cultural, political, and national influences had distorted the religious beliefs of Judaism to the point that they did not even recognize Christ or God's true character and purposes. This same corruption in religious beliefs is also the foundational theme of the New Testament Epistles, making it worthy of every Christian disciple's intentional study.

Finally, two areas of this study may be somewhat new to some: hearing the voice of God and journaling. God speaks to His people in many different ways. Some hear an audible voice, others through their own conscience, and still others through their thoughts. The point is that the Scriptures tell us He does speak to His people. By reading the listed Scriptures and listening, you are telling yourself and God that you do believe He will speak to you personally. When the God of the universe speaks to you, it must be of extreme importance and worth writing down for future reference. Journaling may seem difficult and trivial at first, but the experience of those who journal testifies to its value when entries are revisited after a period of time. Journaling is invaluable in measuring personal spiritual growth. Where would we be today without the Gospels, the disciples' journal of their time spent with Christ?

May God's grace, peace, and love rest abundantly on those who undertake this study.

FAITH

Faith is being sure of what we hope for and certain of what we do not see…without faith it is impossible to please God. (Hebrews 11:1, 6)

Scripture reading:

Hebrews 11:1–12:2; John 11:25–26; 14:1–4; Luke 18:1–8

(While reading, watch for anything God is revealing, and record God's revelations and your response in your belief journal.)

At the heart of today's Scriptures are the terms faith and believing in God. At times they almost seem to be interchangeable, and yet as simple thoughts in our heads, they have a powerful influence over how we live. Like music, they move us. So to aid our understanding, let's use music as a tangible analogy. Consider faith as an orchestra, where all the different musical instruments represent beliefs. Hebrews 12:2 states that "Jesus is the author and perfecter of our faith."

Therefore, in this analogy Jesus becomes the conductor. Note how the different instruments (beliefs) are organized into groups: woodwind, brass, percussion, and string. In each of these groups, there is a hierarchy, yet they sound with an organized oneness at the direction of the conductor. Jesus tunes, sets the tempo, and arranges the dynamics of the different groups so as to perform the symphony written by God, the composer. Just as the instruments of an orchestra are able to come together as one dynamic in a symphony, so likewise our beliefs come together in our hearts to create faith in God through Jesus—a faith attitude that is able to influence our thoughts, emotions, and obedience as Christ's disciples in how we hope, love, trust, obey, and serve.

With this analogy in mind, reread Hebrews 11:1–12:2, with the understanding that faith is a powerful influence that goes beyond just a single belief in God's existence. To the patriarchs of old, faith in God was a living expression of the sum of all their beliefs concerning God's character, promises, and provisions, as well as His love and concern for His creation. As we read, we get a strong sense of how the patriarchs' faith (beliefs) provided them with strong convictions and assurances of who God is even in the face of a culture and situations that were saying differently. The writer of Hebrews tells us that it is this faith in God that enables a believer to confidently trust and obey God with both assurance and expectation. The writer also tells us that these patriarchs were commended by God for their faith, which did not waver even though none of them saw the fulfillment of the promise in their lifetime. Our reading in John provides us faith's promise; we have salvation from sin and eternal life through Christ.

This faith of today's New Testament Christian extends out of the fulfillment of God's Old Testament promises and blessings through His Christ, a faith that the patriarchs only hoped for. It's a living expression of all our beliefs trusting in the person of Jesus as God's Christ, the teaching of the New Testament, and Christ's redemptive work at Calvary. As with the patriarchs, it is a powerful influence in that it brings about a radical and total commitment to Jesus as the Lord of our life. Hebrews 11:40 tells us that this faith is "better" because it is able to make us, along with the patriarchs of old, "perfect." We share with the patriarchs the assurance and expectation that Jesus will return for His own (John14:1–4). In our final reading from Luke, Jesus ponders the persistence of faith and questions whether it will remain until He returns.

Belief and Prayer Journal: Pray that God's grace will enable your persistence in your believing and your faith. Does the music inside you include beliefs that Jesus will return? If you were to describe your faith as God's symphony playing in your heart, what and how would you tell someone about the music?

WEEK 1: THURSDAY

BELIEFS, ATTITUDES, AND CREEDS

**Then they asked him, "What must we do to do the works God requires?" Jesus answered, "The work of God is this: to believe in the one he has sent".
(John 6:28–29)**

Scripture reading:
John 6:26–42; Philippians 2:1–11; Romans 12:1–13; Apostle's Creed
(While reading, watch for anything God is revealing, and record God's revelations and your response in your belief journal.)

Yesterday, with the analogy of an orchestra, we saw how faith in God is the product of everything one believes concerning God's character, promises, and love for His creation. Today, we will look at the process of believing and how beliefs influence our lives as disciples.

5

Beliefs are said to be the simplest of building blocks in the human thinking process. Starting at birth, we begin forming and collecting beliefs concerning things such as our self, family, the world around us, church, and God. By teaching and learning, beliefs are passed from generation to generation through family and church. In our first reading, Jesus is teaching his followers that believing in the spiritual and the divine nature of Christ requires more mental work than the tangible things like miracles, wonders, signs, and their ancestral pedigree. As a disciple, is your desire the emotionality of miracles, signs, and wonders apart from the relationship of believing in Jesus as Lord? As a disciple, are you doing the work of believing?

Now attitudes, both positive and negative, are collections of highly organized beliefs toward either something or someone. They have the ability to influence not only our behaviors but also how we think and feel. Attitudes get this power because we store our beliefs (attitudes) linked to strong memories and powerful emotions: love, joy, trust, hate, fear, and anger. As an example, consider your memories and attitude concerning God. In some, the emotional response may be one of love, joy, or trust, but for others it might be fear or even anger. In our second reading, we learn that as disciples, we should have the same attitude as Jesus—humble, encouraging, tender, compassionate, and like-minded in love and Spirit. Now consider your attitude toward your neighbor. Does your belief attitude match that of Christ, and is it easy for you to put others' needs before your own?

Finally, believing is the mental work or process required to maintain a belief, and it must be continued or the belief will fade away and become unimportant in doubt, unbelief, or disbelief. This mental process (work/learning) is one of collecting information that supports the belief while rejecting any opposition. (Later in our study, we will

6

look at this process as one directed by the Holy Spirit.) The work of believing in the spiritual nature of God and His kingdom is active and not passive. In Romans we learn that it is the basis for our spiritual worship, one which we must do daily by the renewing of our minds in Scripture while not conforming to the patterns or teaching of this world. As a disciple, are you renewing your mind daily with the truth of Scripture under the guidance of the Spirit?

Belief and Prayer Journal: Religious creeds such as the Apostle's Creed are statements of core beliefs that support the Christian Faith. Prayerfully read the Apostle's Creed, stopping at each belief to journal what you really believe. Ask the Spirit's help with any doubt or unbelief. Is your attitude the same as that of Jesus? Pray for God's help in making it such.

UNBELIEF, DOUBT, AND HARDNESS OF THE HEART

See to it, brothers, that none of you has a sinful, unbelieving heart that turns away from the living God.
(Hebrews 3:12)

Scripture reading:
Hebrews 3: 12–19; John 20:24–31; Luke 24:13–35; 2 Timothy 2:11–26;
Mark 9:14–29
(While reading, watch for anything God is revealing, and record God's revelations and your response in your belief journal.)

We began this study with the analogy of the Christian Faith as an orchestra playing the composer God's powerful symphony of love and grace in the believer's heart. In this analogy we looked at how our beliefs concerning God's character, promises, and provision

9

come together like musical instruments under the control of Christ the conductor as they play a moving symphony of saving faith through our lives. Today we will consider the effects of doubt, unbelief, and false beliefs on our Christian Faith. In the above analogy, doubt and unbelief would be like untuned or uncompliant instruments not responding spiritually to Christ as the conductor. False and erroneous beliefs on the other hand would damage our faith symphony much like putting some ukuleles or banjoes in the string section or some kazoos or harmonicas in the wind section. Through this analogy one gets an awesome sense of how God's faith symphony of beliefs could be diminished and distorted by the effects of doubt and unbelief, as well as false beliefs, in the life and service of Christians. What we believe motivates and moves us forward as disciples, while doubt and disbelief only serve to paralyze and keep us dead in our sin.

Yesterday, we learned that believing in the saving grace of God is the required work on the part of Christians. The work of believing is the process in which one makes a decision to believe and then begins collecting Scriptural truth that is supportive of that belief while dispelling any contradictory worldly human knowledge that denies it. Doubting is a failure to work at dispelling worldly contradictory knowledge with the truth of scripture under the guidance of the Holy Spirit. Although to have some doubt is not sin, if it is allowed to linger, collect, and multiply, doubt only hardens the heart as it leads to the sin of unbelief. In our first reading, we learn that it is our responsibility "to be sure" we don't have a sinful unbelieving heart. As for doubt, in our second reading, we see the risen Jesus not commending the disciple Thomas for doubting but reprimanding him to "stop doubting and believe." As for how, we read in our third reading in Luke about the doubting disciples (slow of heart to believe) on the road to Emmaus.

Note how Jesus "opened the Scriptures… beginning with Moses and the prophets" dispelling doubt and disbelief in these disciples causing their hearts to burn with belief and return to the fellowship. As for the effect of false beliefs, we turn to Paul's instructions to Timothy. In it the Spirit cautions us as disciples not to be "ashamed" of Christ while we "correctly handle the word of truth." Note how false beliefs by the ungodly spread like gangrene destroying the faith of some.

Belief and Prayer Journal: As in Mark we too live in a "perverse and unbelieving generation." The father with the sick child knew what he believed as he asked Jesus' help in overcoming doubt and unbelief. In journaling we turn to Scripture and ask for Christ's help. Pray for the Spirit's help to draw you into a love relationship of trust with God's word, the Bible.

REPENTANCE

"…Repent for the kingdom of heaven is near."
(Matthew 4:17)

Scripture reading:
Romans 2:1–11; Ezekiel 18:20–32; Jonah 4:3–10; Revelation 2:4–5
(While reading, watch for anything God is revealing, and record God's revelations and your response in your belief journal.)

Have you ever been following directions to get somewhere and at some point you realize that a while back you zigged when you should have zagged and now you are hopelessly lost? Now there are those who try to view this situation positively and say, "I was just discovering things I didn't intend to see," but you are missing the fact that you are not where you were meant to be. There are also those who say this is a male thing… but, ladies, what about that last recipe you were following? You remember the one which tasted so awful it secretly hit the trash. Following directions no matter what you're doing is important because failure results in consequences. This is never truer than when the directions and the recipes are from God and concern living a righteous life. We want to do the right thing, but more often than not, we fail. Today's scriptures relate to how we fail and sin as individuals, as a nation, and yes as church. They also point to repentance as a means of correction, forgiveness, and restoration.

The Bible speaks of repenting as the process of changing from living a sinful life to that of doing right and living for God. The change has to be so complete as to affect our attitudes, beliefs, and behaviors. Romans 2:1–11 shares with us there is "no excuse" for not having a repentant heart. It tells us not to be "stubborn" by judging others and rejecting the truth of the Bible. The prophet Ezekiel shares with us the fact that no matter how wrong we think we have gone, God is just and fair. If we repent, He will forgive and restore us.

Concerning our nation, the wicked city of Nineveh repented and changed on hearing God's message of punishment through the prophet Jonah. Would God not also do the same for the USA? Finally as church, have we become like the church at Ephesus? Have we become so entangled in the world's ways that we have forsaken our first love and forgotten our mission to make disciples of Christ, teaching them all He taught? Is it time for us to repent as individuals, as church, and as a nation?

Belief and Prayer Journal: Matthew tells us that when Jesus began his preaching, he preached a message of repentance. What do you believe about God and His kingdom? Are God's ways truly just and fair? As people, a nation, and church, is it possible that we are living in an ungodly manner and need to repent? Repentance is not something to treat lightly. It goes beyond a simple "I'm sorry," especially when it concerns something as important as our salvation and eternal life. Pray through the Holy Spirit that God will convict your heart, the heart of our nation, and the heart of His church to acknowledge our fallen condition and help us to repent and become more obedient servants in His kingdom.

THE WALK OF THE CROSS
CHRISTIAN DISCIPLESHIP: DYING TO SELF

What the Bible Says We Should Believe
Sunday: a day for contemplation and focused meditation

We've spent the last four days in the Bible defining and clarifying what the Bible says about belief and faith through the analogy of an orchestra. What we learned will serve as a foundational structure for the weeks ahead on which to build our Christian Faith. Each Sunday we've set aside as a time to look backward and reflect in the Spirit's grace as well as to consider the week ahead. In the coming week, we will be looking at what the Bible says we should believe about God:

Monday: God as Creator
Tuesday: God as Father (Abba) in the Trinity

Wednesday: God as Holy
Thursday: God as Eternal
Friday: God's Grace
Saturday: God's Sabbath Rest

Sunday is considered the Christian Sabbath, and it should be a time for church fellowship as well as resting in God. It is also a great time to contemplate our Lenten "walk of the cross" as we meditate on Jesus' walk of the cross. Often we relate to it only as His last week but it is so much more. The Bible teaches that Jesus' ministry starts some three to four years earlier when He leaves His home town Nazareth and journeys down the fertile Jordan Valley. His destination is the wilderness desert of Judea to visit and be baptized by His cousin John. Yes this is family, and although the Bible doesn't speak about their interaction in youth, why would they not have? From their very births, both had God's finger prints on them and their families. Jesus is baptized by John and receives the Spirit as the Scripture foretold. The Spirit then leads Jesus into the wilderness for forty days of fasting and prayer. It's a time He spends being strengthened in His knowledge and relationship with the Father prior to being tested by Satan. Matthew in Chapters 3 and 4, Mark in Chapter 1, Luke in Chapters 3 and 4, and John in Chapter 1 all come together to provide us with a composite picture of the drama. It was now time for Jesus to put all that He believed about his Father's will for His life on the line as it influences His behavior and His journey through His teaching ministry to the obedience of the cross and beyond. Satan had no power over Him.

As you meditate on how it all began for Jesus, contemplate your personal faith journey and how it begins out of your knowledge of God and His desire for us to have an intimate personal relationship with Himself through Jesus as our Lord, Christ, and King.

GOD AS CREATOR

**In the beginning God created.
(Genesis 1:1)**

Before you read today's scriptures, ask yourself what you really believe about the meaning of life and how it all began.

Scripture reading:
Genesis 1 and 2; John 1:1–14
(While reading, watch for anything God is revealing, and record God's revelations and your response in your belief journal.)

This week we will be looking at what we believe about God's absolute sovereignty and infinite power and what better place to start than with His role as creator and sustainer of life. What was your answer about how life began? The choices are not many. You either believe science's evolution theory or the narration in Genesis of God

19

as the creator and sustainer of life. However, one must be careful not to combine parts of the two because this will only become problematic when it comes to beliefs in the nonphysical: heaven, angels, spirituality and the afterlife. Also, one must keep in mind that *evolution* is random and accidental with no accounting for God, whereas *creation* is divine with willfulness and intentionality. Creation cannot be understood by the scientific method. This belief choice is significant because as we saw last week, God as Creator is a core belief that serves as the foundation for a lot of other beliefs that influence your attitude and how you live your life as a disciple of Christ.

Now that your choice is creation, slowly read the first and second chapters of Genesis as historical events which represent the sovereignty of God and believe how they clearly display that He alone is the creator. Note how some thirty plus times God's infinite power was displayed when God created, God said, God divided, God made, and God saw. Also note God's intentionality and purpose after each act: "and it was so" and "behold it was very good." Our beliefs in creation are important because they help us understand that because God created everything, it belongs to Him and therefore He has the sovereign rights not only to rule over it but to deal with all things as He so desires.

This brings us to our beliefs about mankind's relational role in God's creation and sovereign rule. The second chapter of Genesis is much like an epilog written to provide additional details on God's purpose in creating man in chapter one. In chapter one there is a creation crescendo building up in complexity to God's creating of man. Don't miss the conference between the persons of the Godhead: "let us make man in our image and likeness." It is mentioned nowhere else in creation, and it speaks to our beliefs concerning mankind as the pinnacle of God's creation and our spiritual relationship to Him.

Finally, don't miss why mankind is given dominion (rule) over the other creatures. This structure of man as the highest in creation, standing between God and the rest of creation, represents theocracy. In God's kingdom, God as creator is the sovereign ruler, and by creating man in His image and placing man in the world with dominion makes man a vice-ruler. Yet man does not rule for himself. He rules on behalf of God while acknowledging God as his ruler and creator. Initially creation was perfect without flaw, but man's disobedience brought spiritual death which led to physical death and the need for redemption. The Bible stands as God's redemptive history of mankind as the Old Testament morphs into the New. This brings us to our final reading in John where we read about the "light" of God's redemptive plan Jesus for those who believe and become "children of God."

Belief and Prayer Journal: Is God as "the creator and sustainer of life" a belief in your faith orchestra? Do you need to remove any God-limiting beliefs concerning His sovereignty and power? Are you a child in the Kingdom of God? God's word says His ways are not man's ways. (Isaiah 55:8-9) Pray for Spiritual discernment to aid you in believing in His ways over the world's ways. The world failed and continues to fail at recognizing the light of God that came into it. Are you part of the world or part of the Kingdom of God?

GOD AS FATHER (ABBA) IN THE TRINITY

**He [Jesus] said to them, "When you pray, say:
'Father, hallowed be your name, your kingdom come.
Give us each day our daily bread.'"
(Luke 11: 2–3)**

Scripture reading:
Luke 11:1–13; Genesis 3; Matthew 28:16–20; 2 Thessalonians 2:13–17
(While reading, watch for anything God is revealing, and record God's
revelations and your response in your belief journal.)

In your prayer time, do you call on God as your Father in heaven as
Jesus is teaching in our first reading? Through the relationship of
a Father to his children, Jesus is reframing cultural beliefs about God
from distant and non-caring to that of an intimate Father that desires a

personal relationship as He cares for us as His children. Today, we will look at what we should believe about God in this role of Father in the Trinity and why it is important to Christians.

The Scriptures are full of teaching references concerning relationship role dyads: parent–children, male–female, husband–wife, rabbi (teacher)–student, physician–patient, priest–worshiper, king–servant, and master–slave. What we believe about these roles is important because those beliefs produce expectations in us of what functions we and others should or should not perform in relationships. As Christians we should be vigilant that these beliefs about roles have a biblical core that has not been distorted by the world culture or some past negative personal experience. With that in mind, consider what you believe concerning the function of fatherhood which is part of the parent–child relational role. Do your beliefs align with the Bible's teaching that a father should provide protection, love, care, and provision, as well as spiritual and religious development, to his children? Do your beliefs also include a father's discipline and correction? More importantly, in humility can you assume the role of an obedient child?

Yesterday, in Genesis 1–2 we learned that God as Creator takes on the role of Father to all creation. As Father He created His children Adam and Eve perfect in His image and likeness in the roles of male–female and husband–wife and there was perfect relationship. Today, in Genesis 3 we learn that their disobedience (sin) not only distorted their relationship with God, it also distorted their roles in family. Yet in His discipline, God reveals Himself as a compassionate Father by meeting their needs. He meets their physical needs by clothing them (v 21). As for the penalty of death, He provides the promise of Christ (the offspring of the woman) in the role of savior/redeemer (v 15) for both of them and us as their offspring.

From Genesis 3 concerning the fall of humanity to our sinful nature, the reader gets the first glimpses of the functions contained in the roles of our Triune God. In our final two New Testament readings, the believer gets a fuller understanding of those relational roles. The oneness of the Trinity can be experienced by the believer as God in the role of Creator and Father, Jesus as our King, Redeemer and Savior, and the Holy Spirit as the power to sanctify and sustain.

Belief and Prayer Journal: In response to desires for titles and greatness, Jesus taught disciples it was better to humble themselves to the role of a child (Mathew 18:1–14). Are you able to take on the role of a child as Jesus taught? Intimacy is often contained in role titles. In His most stressing time in the garden, Jesus prayed "Abba," the most intimate title for father (Mark 14:36). It is our equivalent for "papa." How intimate is God the Father in your prayers?

GOD AS HOLY

...be holy in all you do; for it is written:
"Be holy because I am Holy."
(1 Peter 1:15-16)

Scripture reading:
I Peter1:1–16; Ephesians 4:17–32; John 14:15–27
(While reading, watch for anything God is revealing, and record God's
revelations and your response in your belief journal.)

In our opening Scripture, Peter cautions the Christian disciples to
whom he is writing about conforming to the way the rest of the
world lives. He instructs believers not to follow evil desires but to be
holy in all that they do because their God is Holy. As a believer, are you
holy in all that you do? Before you answer, it may help to know what
holy means. The word "holy" as used in the scriptures means being
set apart and belonging to God. Biblically speaking, holy implies the

godly attributes of saintly, sinless, consecrated, reverent, and spiritually perfect. Like all godly attributes, the scripture writer's concern is that the disciple be continually growing and maturing in holiness so as to imitate Christ. Now with that in mind, let's reconsider the question: Does all that you do (or say) set you apart from the world and reverence God? Also, are you striving to be holy and are you maturing in holiness? This devotional is designed to encourage belief in the desire to grow and mature in holiness as Christ's disciples and as His church.

If you are like most believers, the above questions make you feel uncomfortable because they produce the Holy Spirit's convictions concerning your inadequacies. Peter tells us we are to live as "strangers in the world." Believers are to live a life of "new birth" in obedience and self-control with our minds set on Christ. In our second reading, Paul insists that believers not live like the world that has lost "all sensitivity" to God because they have turned themselves over to the world's sensuality and indulgences. Paul goes on to tell believers that they know the "truth of Jesus" and that the ways of their former life were corrupted by deceitful desires. He tells believers that they were taught to "put off the old self" and be the "new self" that God created. In so doing, believers will be "like God in true righteousness and holiness." Paul ends this second reading with a list of worldly behaviors to be put off because they grieve the Holy Spirit of God. Instead we should be compassionate, forgiving, and building each other up as to imitate Christ.

In our final reading, Jesus assures believers that living the spiritual life is possible with the help of the Holy Spirit who lives within believers, helping and teaching obedience to God. Jesus tells believers that the world cannot accept the Spirit because it neither sees Him nor knows Him.

Belief and Prayer Journal: Living spiritually and serving Christ require dying to the self's desires and living separately from this world. In all the Gospels (Mathew 16:24–26; Mark 8:34–38; Luke 9:23–26; John 12:25–26), Jesus told His disciples they must lose, forfeit, deny, and die to "self." Are your beliefs in line with Christ's? Journal both your weakness and strengths while asking the Holy Spirit to help you to daily die to self and grow in holiness to be more like Christ. Pray, asking the Spirit to help you become more holy because our God is holy.

GOD AS ETERNAL

[Jesus prayed] "Now this is eternal life: that they may know you, the only true God, and Jesus Christ, whom you have sent."
(John 17:3)

Scripture reading:
Genesis 3:17–24; Isaiah 25:6-9, 26:19; I Corinthians 15:1-58;
John 17:1–5
(While reading, watch for anything God is revealing, and record God's revelations and your response in your belief journal.)

When someone loses something of value and discovers it is missing, they normally return to the place they had it last to start a search. As for mankind, the thing of value missing is eternal life through an intimate relationship with God. As for where we had it last, the Scripture plainly tells us it was in the Garden of Eden. For that reason, we will begin our study in Genesis. From there, we will trace the threads of belief through the Old and New Testaments in an attempt to develop a secure Christian faith about the believer's future.

Earlier this week in Genesis 1and 2, we learned that God as our Father and Creator made everything "very good" (perfect) and at the pinnacle of His work He created mankind in His own image. The implication here is that mankind shares a likeness to his Creator to the point mankind is given dominion over all the other living creatures answering only to the Creator. Now since we believe that God is immortal and eternal (I Timothy 1:17), one would assume that mankind was created immortal with eternal existence in relationship with their Creator. If this were not the case why would there be any punishment in death from sin or banishment from intimacy of relationship with God as we read in our first reading? In fact, the fall and loss in Genesis 3 provides the Christian with the reasoning behind many of the doctrinal beliefs of our faith. There is recognition of the "original sin" with its penalty of death which points to a need for "repentance," "atonement," "sanctification," "justification," "redemption," and "salvation" all by God alone in Christ. We also read about the corruption in the "image of God" in mankind which must go through a process of Spiritual "regeneration." Finally there was a distortion in the relationship where mankind needs Jesus (seed of a woman) as the path to "reconciliation" and a future with our God.

Also, when considering what you believe about eternal life, don't miss the Bible's poetic symbolism to help you form those mental images that are so important in maintaining beliefs—symbols like "the tree of life" used in Genesis 3, "the book of life" (Philippians 4:3), "heavenly home" (2 Corinthians 5:1), and the one of a "final banquet in Christ's Kingdom" as described in our reading in Isaiah. Through the imagery of a great feast, we read that our God will swallow up death and wipe away all the tears from pain of suffering forever. In closing, as Christians our belief concerning eternal life (immortality) is more than just survival of the soul without a body. In fact our last two scriptures serve to weave those treads of belief into a beautiful tapestry of the Christian's future—a gift from God of endless existence in communion with Christ much like what was lost in the Garden of Eden. Only this time Paul shares with us that those being saved will inherit a "spiritual body" that is "imperishable" and "incorruptible" bearing the likeness of Jesus as it is empowered by His Spirit forever. The assurance and trustworthiness of this belief is found in Jesus' prayer as recorded by John at the opening of today's study. Life eternal is the gift of a personal relationship where the believer knows God through knowing Jesus and it will exist forever.

Belief and Prayer Journal: A core belief in the Apostles' Creed says, "I believe… in the resurrection of the body and life everlasting." 1 Corinthians 15 could be called Christianity 101. Journal about what the Spirit shares concerning your witness concerning the future of the faith. There is always anxiety over what happens at one's death. Yet to the Christian it's only a gateway to a beginning. Pray for help overcoming your unbelief of an eternal future.

God's Grace

**"My grace is sufficient for you, for my power
is made perfect in weakness."
(2 Corinthians 12:9)**

Scripture reading:
Matthew 20:1–16; Luke 23:32–43; Ephesians 2:1–10;
2 Corinthians 6:1–16
(While reading, watch for anything God is revealing, and record God's
revelations and your response in your belief journal.)

If someone were to ask you about God's saving grace, what would
you tell them? Would you tell them about His loving-kindness,
mercy, and goodwill toward believers? Like Paul, could you also tell
them of the sufficiency of grace and how it is an unmerited free gift
given in abundance through Jesus? In the first reading of the parable of
the workers in the vineyard, Jesus teaches us that we cannot calculate

35

the grace of God as one would calculate daily earnings. The person who comes to God at the end of their life enjoys the same level and quality of His grace as the person who comes in early childhood. As evidence of this, consider God's grace to the thief on the cross next to Jesus in our reading in Luke. Take note of how, as convicted criminals, both thieves deserved punishment and yet only the one who, out of humility, acknowledges God and requests forgiveness receives grace. Luke puts in writing Jesus' reply to the remorseful thief: today you will be with me in paradise. Both Scriptures attest to the fact that God's grace is unmerited, unearned, and even undeserved, and yet His loving-kindness is freely extended to all.

In Paul's epistle to the Ephesians, we read how God's grace does what we are unable to do—save ourselves from who we are and from our iniquity (sin and transgressions). God's grace makes us "alive in Christ" as a gift from God so no one can boast of their good works. Yet note how the believers in Corinth were in danger of receiving God's grace in vain. By fellowshipping with an unbelieving world culture, they were missing the personal relationship with Christ and replacing it with unbelief and works.

Both St. Augustine and John Wesley used the Latin term "prevenient" to describe God's grace. Prevenient means "irresistible." Both St. Augustine and John Wesley believed that God made His saving grace so irresistible that individuals could not refuse. What do you believe about God's grace? Have you been resisting it by avoiding a personal relationship with Jesus? As a disciple, do you believe in His unmerited and undeserved kindness to people to the point that, in your quest to be like Christ, you are kind to others? Or, is your grace to others only "random acts of kindness"? The title Scripture attests to the fact that, like us, Paul lived in the world and suffered from life's problems and ailments. Yet, when God did not take away his affliction after three requests, Paul believed that God's grace was sufficient. It was Paul's weakness that allowed for God's power to be perfectly manifested in his life.

Belief and Prayer Journal: Pray, asking God to reveal the issues in your life where His grace would suffice. Pray also that He teach you and help you to abundantly extend grace to others.

GOD'S SABBATH REST

..."The Sabbath was made for man, not man for the Sabbath.
So the Son of Man is Lord even of the Sabbath."
(Mark 2:27-28)

Scripture reading:
Genesis 1–2:3; Exodus 20:3–11, 31:13–18; Matthew 11:25–12:14;
Hebrews 4:1–16
(While reading, watch for anything God is revealing, and record God's
revelations and your response in your belief journal.)

I n our culture it is not uncommon to hear sayings such as "shop 'til
you drop," "work hard, play harder," and "leave everything on the
field." They capture the idea of expending everything while holding
nothing back to the point of total exhaustion to accomplish our goals.
It is much like how we see God creating the earth and heavens in our
first reading. The reading ends by telling us that after six days, God

deemed creation "very good" and then He ceased creating and rested on the seventh day. God not only rested, He also set aside the seventh day, blessed it for mankind, and made it Holy by setting it apart for Himself. In Judaism this seventh day is called Sabbath because in Aramaic the word for "cease" or "rest" translates to Sabbath. At this point, prior to man's fall into sin, humanity was to experience Sabbath as a relationship of resting in God's intimate care. However, the book of Genesis goes on to tell of sin's increase after man's fall to the point of Israel, His chosen, becoming the slave of Egypt.

With the increase of sin and man's depravity came the Mosaic Law. In our readings in Exodus, we learn how God delivered His chosen people and gave them the Mosaic Law to point their hearts to God's righteousness. In this reading, God reaffirms the Sabbath Rest as the fourth of the Ten Commandments. The seriousness of the command is emphasized in that God considers keeping the Sabbath Rest now a covenantal promise and an outward sign for generations to come in Judaism. Not to remember and practice a Sabbath Rest was paramount to rejecting God. Yet, by the time of Christ, Sabbath was no longer about a relationship of Resting-in-God. Man-made legal rules (Talmud) concerning the keeping of Sabbath made it a burden on people. This legalistic burden put on the people by the religious leaders is the reason behind Jesus' remarks of our opening verse. In them we learn that as in Genesis, the Sabbath was made for man, not man for the Sabbath, and that Jesus was Lord of Sabbath. In Matthew we read that as Lord of the Sabbath, Jesus calls all those who are under heavy burden to come to and find their rest in Him.

Our final reading from Hebrews brings our beliefs full circle. Rest and Salvation cannot be earned through our labor of keeping the Law, special holidays, Sabbath, or any other attempts at being good. Rest and salvation come when we hear the call of God and enter into our Lord's Sabbath Rest through a personal relationship. Later in our study on Jesus, we will learn how He as our Lord and Savior paid the price of Redemption for our souls and His church. In the Gospels, Jesus asks "what is lawful to do on the Sabbath?" His teaching was for disciples to remove the legalism and replace it with a personal relationship with God.

Belief and Prayer Journal: What we do is a reflection of what we believe. Never is this exemplified more than in what we believe about Sunday the Lord's Day. Does your Sunday honor the relationship you have with God through Christ? Have you entered into Christ's rest, or are you still laboring to earn your salvation? Is the Lord's Day a day of worship with fellow Christians (church)? At day's end, are you physically, emotionally, and spiritually rested for the service week ahead? Pray to the Holy Spirit, asking Lord Jesus to show you how to spiritually enrich your relationship with Him as the Church.

THE WALK OF THE CROSS
CHRISTIAN DISCIPLESHIP: DYING TO SELF

What the Bible Says We Should Believe
Sunday: a day for contemplation and focused meditation

We've spent this past week looking at what the Bible says we should believe about God. The constraint of time only allowed us to look at six of His many character traits. So, we chose six pertaining to the role and relationship He has with His creation. Not only is God creator, he is also our eternal Father who sustains and cares for us with loving grace. Because we are created in His image, He has an expectation of believers to be holy as He is holy and for us to enter into His divine rest which He provides. Keep in mind these attributes of God are only but a few which the Bible says are worthy to believe in. Like any intimate relationship, the more we learn, know, and believe, the more we are able to trust. Sunday is our time to look to the week ahead with expectations of what the Bible says we should believe—the week ahead is about Jesus:

Monday: Salvation – Jesus as Our Savior
Tuesday: Redemption – Jesus as Redeemer
Wednesday: Jesus as Our Justification
Thursday: Jesus as the Son of God
Friday: Jesus as Lord
Saturday: "I Am" – Jesus as Divine and Eternal

Remember Sunday is by tradition the Christian Sabbath and, although believers are not mandated, it should be a time for church fellowship as well as a Sabbath Rest in God. It is also a good time to review the past week's journal as we consider what lies ahead in our Lenten study of the walk of the cross. Last Sunday we contemplated Jesus' relationship to the Father, His baptism, testing, and His Spiritual connection to God. John the Baptist not only prepared the way, he validated Jesus as the long-expected Messiah with baptism. Under full obedience to God's Spirit, Jesus heads back north to Galilee, and after John's arrest by Herod, Jesus begins His public ministry, preaching and teaching the good news of the coming Kingdom of God, all of which is being validated by the Spirit with signs, wonders, healings, and miracles. A big part of Jesus' work is the ever ongoing calling and commissioning of disciples—those called to be a living copy of Jesus. It started with the original twelve (Matt.10:1-18) and then the commissioning of the seventy (Luke 10:1-20) and then the great commission (Matt. 28:18-20) for us all. In His training of disciples, the Gospels tell us that Jesus would often challenge disciples by asking do you not have eyes to see, ears to hear, and a heart to understand? Today's meditation is on Jesus' call of discipleship on your life. After considering the cited Scriptures, contemplate your personal faith journey of walking in the footsteps of the Master. Afterward, spend time thanking God and asking for eyes to see, ears to hear, and a heart to understand.

SALVATION: JESUS AS OUR SAVIOR

**She will give birth to a son, and you (Joseph) are to give him
the name Jesus, because he will save his
people from their sins.
(Matthews 1:21)**

Scripture reading:
Isaiah 7:13–14, 9:6–7; Matthew 1:1–25; Luke 1–2:40
(While reading, watch for anything God is revealing, and record God's
revelations and your response in your belief journal.)

In his play *Romeo and Juliet*, William Shakespeare asked the poignant question: what's in a name? His point was that a rose by any other name would smell as sweet and still be a rose. It's the idea of looking past a name to the attributes associated with it. This idea is extremely helpful in the study of Scripture because, to the ancients, naming something was more important than just a label. A name was to provide an outward descriptive meaning. In the case of a child, it directed and distinguished the child as they lived their life. On that same note, if there was a major change in direction of one's life, it was usually represented with a change to the person's name, such as Jacob was renamed Israel, Simon renamed Peter, and Saul took the name Paul.

However, some care needs to be taken when reading biblical names because the ancients employed a variety of methods in naming their children. Some chose names that represented animals and natural objects such as Jonah meaning "dove" and Tamar meaning "palm tree." Others chose names that reflected a physical characteristic of the child at birth: Esau meaning he was "hairy" from birth. Another method of choosing a child's name was to connect it with some incident at their birth. Abraham's wife Rachel as she was dying in childbirth named her son Ben-oni or "son of my pain", which Abraham later changed to Benjamin meaning "son of my right hand." Finally, there was the method of prophetic utterance concerning the child's future in their name: Dan meaning "judge" foretold of a future of judging people. This brings us to our first reading in Isaiah, God's prophet to Ahaz king of Judah, and the prophetic name of Jesus.

Now, Ahaz as king did evil by leading God's people into sin, idolatry, social injustice, and child sacrifice. Isaiah had the task of prophesying to Ahaz not only God's righteous judgments and punishment but a message of a future King who would provide redemption and salvation for God's people. Ahaz, in disbelief, was told the timing would be marked by a "sign" of a virgin giving birth and naming the child Emmanuel meaning "God with us." From there we move some

700 plus years into the future to our two Gospel readings concerning the fulfillment of those prophesies. In them, Joseph and Mary were instructed by an angel that Mary's virgin birth was Emmanuel "God with us" and they were to give the child the prophetic name of Jesus.

So what is in the name of Jesus? More than can be written about here, yet several things would top the list. Firstly, Jesus is the fulfillment of the promise of Emmanuel, where God took on human flesh and entered history being both human and divine. Secondly, Jesus is both the Christ and Messiah, meaning "anointed by God" for the purpose of office. The offices of King, Priest, and Prophet were all commissioned by God with the anointing of scented oil. Jesus was anointed by God with the oil of the Holy Spirit to be King, Priest, and Prophet. Finally, His prophetic name Jesus means "God saves." Jesus, through the example of the life He lived and His redemptive work on the cross, brought forgiveness and salvation from sin and death, thus bringing restoration and peace with God to those who believe.

Belief and Prayer Journal: The name Jesus means Priest, King, Lord, Savior, Redeemer, Messiah, and Christ. Our individual beliefs in His descriptive names allow us to experience Jesus personally as they deepen our faith. Journal concerning which name contains the most meaning to you. Pray for the Spirit's help to witness to someone concerning your personal experience to one of the names of Jesus as it relates to your life.

REDEMPTION: JESUS AS REDEEMER

**The Lord redeems His servants; no one will
be condemned who takes refuge in him.
(Psalm 34:22)**

Scripture reading:
Genesis 3; Hebrews 9:11–10:10; Romans 8:1–17
(While reading, watch for anything God is revealing, and record God's
revelations and your response in your belief journal.)

Are you a person who saves by redeeming store coupons? Maybe
you are from the generation that was fond of collecting S&H
Green Stamps and later redeeming them for valuable merchandise.
You may even have known someone who temporarily pawned their
valuables only to later redeem them at an exuberant price. Today's

study on "redeeming" asks this question: Do you believe that the Lord has redeemed you? If so, what are you redeemed from and what was the ransom price of your redemption?

Redeeming by definition is the act of recovering ownership by paying a price or a ransom. In the Bible, it represented the Hebrew practice of "buying back" land, a servant, or a kinsman from peril or bondage. It also refers to part of God's saving activity of the Jews and us through Christ as our Redeemer. Redemption, along with words such as deliverance, salvation, and sacrificial atonement, is a role term that helps the believer understand their relationship with God regarding issues such as afflictions, troubles, injustices, self-centeredness, wickedness, evil, sin, and death. Each role term offers the disciple a set of beliefs that will enrich and strengthen their Christian Faith.

Redemption focuses on Christ buying back believers from the curse of the law of sin and death. Genesis 3 tells of the consequences of Adam and Eve's disobedience and betrayal of God's authority and will. This betrayal put mankind between God and His justice and holiness. In order for God's forgiveness to occur, God's anger needed to be appeased (propitiated) and their disobedience (sin) needed to be atoned (expatiated) by a blood sacrifice. They knew God's law—you will surely die (Gen. 2:17). Their fall into disobedience (sin) set into place God's law. In our reading in Hebrews, we learn that "without the shedding of blood, there is no forgiveness." We also learn that Christ's sacrificial shed blood was better than any animal sacrifice and sufficient for God to forgive our "sins and lawless acts." The price Christ paid was so sufficient that no longer was there even a need for a sin sacrifice. It was Christ himself who said "if the Son sets you free, you will be free indeed" (John 8:36). In Romans we read about this new freedom in the Spirit of the Son of God. We learn that as believers we are no longer controlled by our sinful natures; however, this freedom comes with an obligation to belong to Christ who redeemed us.

Belief and Prayer Journal: In your relationship with Jesus, is He your Lord and Redeemer? As for your "obligation," do you allow Him to be your Lord and Master? Who decides the issues of your life? The price of redemption is a two-sided sword with a point. Those on the prideful, arrogant side believe that they are good and don't require His price. Those on the fatalist lost side don't believe that any price is sufficient, including Jesus. In the middle is the point—we all sin and all fall short, needing Christ's redemption and salvation. (Romans 3:23) Pray and meditate on Psalm 51. Allow the Holy Spirit to speak to your heart.

Jesus as Our Justification

Therefore, since we have been justified through faith, we have peace with God through our Lord Jesus Christ.
(Romans 5:1)

Scripture reading:
Romans 3:21–26; Romans 4
(While reading, watch for anything God is revealing, and record God's revelations and your response in your belief journal.)

To be justified means to be made right. Some might say if we are justified, it is just as if we never sinned. But how can this be? Scripture is very clear that all have sinned and fall short of the glory of God (Romans 3:23). It is Romans 5:1 that provides us with the answer. We have been *justified through faith*. God knew that human beings are slaves to sin and are incapable of perfectly obeying His law. Out of His love for His creation, He provided the way to accomplish everything required for our justification.

That of course was the sacrifice of Jesus Christ on the cross, where Jesus gave his blood to pay the price for our justification. Simply by believing and placing our faith in Christ as our Lord and Savior, we are justified—made right with God in a relationship that will last for all eternity.

Do you ever second-guess your salvation, wondering if you will be in heaven some day? Do you ever wonder if there is something else you need to do to ensure you will spend eternity in the presence of God? Ask yourself this question: If God provided the way of justification through faith in Christ, what could we as sinful humans possibly do that would surpass that? Jesus himself stated, "I am the way and the truth and the life. No one comes to the Father except through me" (John 14:6). There is nothing apart from faith in Christ that we need to, or could, do. Psalm 46:10 tells us to "Be still, and know that I am God." That usually makes us think of sitting quietly without moving. The Hebrew word for still means to *cease striving*, giving the image of dropping our hands and doing nothing. If you are working to be justified in God's eyes, try being still. Cease striving, drop your hands, do nothing, and humbly allow the Holy Spirit to flood you with the peace that comes with the knowledge that God, through Christ, has done everything that needs to be done.

Belief and Prayer Journal: What do you believe about justification? Is it possible that through faith in Christ, we could be "just as if we never sinned"? Do you truly believe that Christ's sacrifice is all-sufficient for our justification, or do you believe we must continue to try to earn our way into heaven? Do you believe that no one comes to God except through Christ? If you struggle with believing that you are justified and saved, spend some time in prayer asking God to help you to experience the assurance of your salvation. If you experience the joy of your salvation in a very real way, spend some time in prayer thanking God that He has given you this assurance in and through Christ.

Jesus as the Son of God in the Trinity

**I tell you the truth, the Son can do nothing by himself;
he can only do what he sees his Father doing, because whatever the Father does the Son also does.
(John 5:19)**

Scripture reading:
John 5; John 1:43–51; Psalm 8; Daniel 7:13–14; Matthew 21:1–11; Galatians 3:26–4:7
(While reading, watch for anything God is revealing, and record God's revelations and your response in your belief journal.)

Have you ever heard the old idiom "Like father like son"? We often use it when the personality or actions of a child put us in mind of the child's father. At thirty plus years of age, Jesus is certainly not a child, but the idiom serves well here in our first reading. It captures Jesus' defense of His "Sonship" to the pharisaic Jews who were persecuting Him for breaking laws of the Sabbath by healing. Now, the Jews of Jesus' day experienced God quite differently than believers do in our era of Church. They understood in a prideful way that as Jews, they were a chosen people of God, and yet with the Mosaic Law and their ever-growing political and legalistic structure, they were depersonalizing the very God who chose them. As Jews they had replaced their mission of seeking the lost with rules and traditions that only distanced God from the people. In the context of all this Judaism, Jesus offered them a revelation of a compassionate, personal, and healing God who loved the world to the extent of sending His one and only Son as Redeemer-Savior (John 3:16). The ideas of Jesus calling God His "Father" and eternal life only coming through the Son infuriated the Jews as it upset their legalism, yet those ideas are the very beliefs that serve as the core in the Christian Faith. Today we will be looking at what the Christian should believe about the three facets of Jesus' Sonship: Son of God, Son of man, and Son of David.

Son of God—In our first reading, we see this as Jesus' Divine title as it links Him to the Trinity, not in equality but in a relationship of unity called Sonship. Through this relationship the Son is loved, empowered, and entrusted with judgment and destiny by the Father to do the will of the Father. The Father's will is Jesus' mission of atonement, death, resurrection, and Second Advent.

Son of man—As can be seen in our next reading in John, this is the title Jesus preferred. He used it most when referring to Himself throughout the Gospels. It links Jesus to His humanity with assurances that He understands the needs, thoughts, and ways of mankind (Psalm 8). Through His birth He was made like His brothers in every way

(Hebrews 2:17) and therefore is qualified to judge humanity because He belongs to it. The title also links Him to Old Testament prophesy of Daniel and Ezekiel where humanity relies on God's spiritual power.

Son of David—This is Jesus' Jewish title linking Him to the Kingdom. In our reading in Matthew, we see it used as His Messianic title describing His triumphal entry into Jerusalem. As a humble gentle King, He is fulfilling the Davidic covenant in that Jesus will sit on the throne of Israel forever —"Hosanna to the Son of David" meant he is being praised as a saving King.

The importance of what a Christian should believe about the Sonship of Jesus is found in our final reading in Galatians. In it we learn we are all sons of God through Jesus because God has sent the Spirit of His son into our hearts. Things like gender, race, societal position, and worldly methods to separate us are all lost in God's gift through the rights of Sonship.

Belief and Prayer Journal: Did you notice above how the legalism and traditions of practicing religion trapped the Jews into earning their way to God? Through Sonship with the Christ, God offers the priceless gift of forgiveness, salvation, and eternal life. Journal about what God is saying to you about avoiding your religious practices to earn His Love. Pray for the Spirit's help to change those religious practices into a personal relational experience with Jesus through Sonship.

WEEK 3: FRIDAY

JESUS AS LORD

**Why do you call me, 'Lord, Lord', and do not do what I say?
(Luke 6:46)**

Scripture reading:
Luke 6:20–49; Matthew 5, 6, 7
(While reading, watch for anything God is revealing, and record God's
revelations and your response in your belief journal.)

Have you ever experienced issues over obedience? They could
be with getting your children, family members, students,
employees, or even a pet to obey the rules. Or, it could be your own
unwillingness, for whatever reason, to obey the rules of someone in
authority above you. Now, some may think disobedience is a healthy
outcome of self-reliance, while others think it is a product of this me-
centered Western culture. Yet last week we studied this same nature of
disobedience to authority in Adam and Eve. In fact, the Bible recounts

61

a litany of peoples and nations between us and them who also share in this unhealthy nature and its resulting consequences. *Consequences:* therein lies the problem with disobedience, which brings us to our readings concerning Jesus as our LORD.

Let's begin with the title "Lord, Lord" which Jesus employs as His title in this teaching. The power of a role is in the title. In the role of Lord, power is established within the details and levels of authority of the relationship. Now, any good Bible dictionary will define "lord" as a person having great power and authority such as a king, ruler, owner, teacher, or master. It will also address the fact that the Bible uses the word in two ways: as a title of honor and authority in human relationships or as a divine title for Jehovah as God. Now, the question is not which way Jesus was employing the term; He knew His Divinity. The question is how those hearing, which includes us, understand His choice of title. Is Jesus only a good teacher to be honored, or is He the Savior King in the Jehovah God Trinity, thus mandating obedience? Either decision comes with the additional question of what to do with the teaching and/or the consequence associated with disobedience.

As with all biblical teaching, it is important to keep things in context. In so doing, immediately after the above teaching on the Beatitudes from the Sermon on the Mount, Jesus provides two helpful parables: "A tree and its fruit" and "The wise or foolish builder." This teaching is so fundamentally different from the traditional teaching on Jewish legalism it had to produce questions—the same questions we need to answer today when we read these verses. Who is this Jesus and what authority is His teaching based on? How or why should we respond? Thus the parables help people understand Jesus as Lord and our relationship of obedience to His authority in doing the Will of

God. Anything else had the consequence of destruction and not gaining access into the Kingdom of God (heaven).

In closing, in Matthew 7:21–23, Jesus shares concerns over those who honor His name and title while lacking the experience of a personal relationship with Him. Then as today, people often do things for a good cause to honor a person's name. Such are those who will say to Jesus on the Day of Judgment we did things in "Your" name to earn access to the Kingdom, to which He will reply, be gone I never "knew" you. Access to the Kingdom of God is predicated on a personal relationship with Jesus where in intimacy we know Him as Lord as we are known by Him as obedient in doing not our will, but the will of God.

Belief and Prayer Journal: Have you bowed a knee and submitted to the authority of Jesus as your Lord and King? Journal about what holds you back from giving Him your total obedience while allowing His Spirit to conform your character to Jesus' teachings. Pray for the Spirit's help so as to change the focus of your beliefs from who you think you are to His will and Kingdom.

"I AM": JESUS AS DIVINE AND ETERNAL

**"I tell you the truth," Jesus answered,
"before Abraham was born, I am!"
(John 8:58)**

Scripture reading:
Exodus 3:1–14; John 8:48–59; 6:35–41; 8:12; 9:1–7; 10:1–21; 11:1–44
(While reading, watch for anything God is revealing, and record God's
revelations and your response in your belief journal.)

We've spent the week looking at what the Scriptures say we
should believe about Jesus. We read about His "Sonship" in
the Trinity along with a multitude of descriptive titles such as Savior,
Christ, Redeemer, Justifier, Lord, and King. All of these should affirm
core beliefs in the Christian's faith system. Today, we will read and study

the most important of all beliefs: those pertaining to Jesus' Divine and Eternal nature. We will do this by following Jesus' "I Am" declarations that John weaves through the tapestry of his Gospel about Jesus.

Now, Jesus' usage of "I Am" needs to be understood in the context of the beliefs and practices of Judaism. This takes us to our first reading in Exodus where Moses at the burning bush desires to know the name of God. God replies "I Am who I Am" or in Hebrew "Yahweh." Scholars tell us that Yahweh is the third-person form of a verb meaning "he is" or "he will be." More simply put, when we speak of God, we say "He is," yet when God speaks of himself, He says "I Am." Therefore, Yahweh represents God not only as divine and always present but personal, intimate, and covenantal. However, there are several other facts in this first reading that will help us understand the beliefs of Judaism. The first is that Yahweh is the God of their forefathers, Moses, Abraham, Isaac, and Jacob. Next, God entered history to bring the Israelites out of the slavery and oppression in Egypt to a good land to worship Him in freedom. Finally, and most important, "I Am" is to be God's name forever, and the Jews were to remember it from generation to generation.

This brings us to our first reading in John where Jesus publicly declares Himself to be "I Am" and before both the genealogy and the Mosaic Law of the Jews. To those listening and to us, Jesus' declaration of "I Am" is a clear statement that He is God. However, John does not stop there. He goes on to share seven other "I Am" declarations of Jesus in his Gospel. Through them Jesus connects those listening with a God who cares, loves, provides, and is full of grace. The first is "I am the bread of life" (John 6:35) to those who experienced the miraculous feeding and wanted more. Second, to a healed blind man and to all who are Spirituality blind, Jesus affirmed, "I am the light of the world" (John 8:12; 9:5). Later to the common people who labored in menial jobs like that of the shepherds, Jesus said, "I am the gate" and also "I am the good shepherd" (John 10:7; 10:11). In these statements, Jesus was using figurative language representing God's faithfulness, guidance, and protection as the prophetic Messiah who would shepherd God's people. Later, John recounts Jesus comforting Lazarus' sisters and others who were mourning. Prior to raising Lazarus back to life, Jesus said, "I am the resurrection and the life" (John11:25). It was the promise of eternal life and a message of comfort to them and to us.

Finally, John shares with us two final affirmations of Jesus as "I Am." In His final hours, Jesus desired to comfort and calm the anxiety of His disciples by telling us: "I am the way, the truth and the life" (John 14:6). The next was "I am the vine and you are the branches" (John 15:5). This was a metaphor designed to encourage and give hope. As disciples we are branches and if we remain in Him, we will be cared for by the Father and we will bear lasting spiritual fruit.

Belief and Prayer Journal: As you read the above "I Am" affirmations, to which do you relate more? Journal about why the Spirit is drawing you toward it. It may require the work of a belief change. Ask the Spirit's Help to believe fully in Jesus as the great "I Am."

THE WALK OF THE CROSS
CHRISTIAN DISCIPLESHIP: DYING TO SELF

What the Bible Says We Should Believe
Sunday: a day for contemplation and focused meditation

We've spent this past week looking at what the Bible says we should believe about Jesus, what it means to know that Jesus is our Lord and Savior, and what it also means to know Him as our Redeemer who took our penalty for sin to justify believers so that we could be part of the family in the presence of a holy God. We ended the week with beliefs about unity and oneness of Jesus in the Kingdom and in the Trinity. That brings us to the week ahead and what the Bible says we should believe about the third person in the Trinity—the Holy Spirit:

Monday: The Spirit's Regeneration
Tuesday: Sanctification: The Work of the Spirit

Wednesday: The Holy Spirit in the Trinity and in the Believer
Thursday: The Spirit as the Believer's Counselor and Empowerment
Friday: Living by the Spirit and Spiritual Fruit
Saturday: Jesus' Revelation of the Multifunctional Holy Spirit

Sunday, whether you consider it church, fellowship, or by the Greek word *koinonia*, the Bible is explicit—believers in Christ should come together in love, faith, and encouragement (Philippians 2:1–2). Hopefully you have spent time worshiping God in such a fellowship today. This is our day for rest as well as a time to review the past week's journal as we contemplate what lies ahead in our study of Jesus' walk of the cross. So far we have looked at Jesus' Spiritual relationship to Father, baptism, and testing. From there we began to consider His public ministry of preaching, teaching, and miraculous healings. We also saw that a huge part of this ministry was calling and commissioning disciples like us to spread the good news of the coming Kingdom of God. Unfortunately, the advancing of the Kingdom was not all positive. It had its negative resistance with times of unbelief. It starts when Jesus returns to His hometown Nazareth where in the synagogue He reads Isaiah's prophesy about the Messiah restoring sight, healing the lame, and setting the captives free (Luke 4:16–30; Mark 6:1–6; Matthew 13:54–58). What follows is unbelief that the carpenter's son whose brothers and sisters still live there is in fact God's Messiah. Our next scriptures tell us that even Jesus' mother and brothers had doubts and wanted to take charge of Him thinking He had mental issues (Matt.12:46–50; John 7:3–5). Yet what was most distressing was that even some of His own disciples deserted when the teaching took on sacrificial ideas like the body and blood of Christ (John 6:60). It is important in our walk of the cross and discipleship that we keep things in perspective. Discipleship as the walk of the cross and following Jesus as Master and God's Messiah is a walk that is sure to be filled with grief and suffering when we see the world through the Lord's eyes. Read, study, and meditate on Isaiah 53, and then contemplate your expectation of discipleship.

THE SPIRIT'S REGENERATION

**No one can enter the Kingdom of God
unless he is born of water and the spirit.
(John 3:5)**

Scripture reading:
Genesis 3:1–24; Romans 5:12–21; John 3:1–21; Titus 3:1–8
(While reading, watch for anything God is revealing, and record God's
revelations and your response in your belief journal.)

Have you ever lost an important document like a birth certificate,
a passport, or a license? This type of loss often occurs in times
of catastrophes like floods, fires, or break-ins. Yet, it may also happen
when you try to retrieve a valuable electronic file and are greeted with
the message: file is lost or corrupted and cannot be opened. When
things like this happen, we are faced with the painful process of "regenerating" what is lost. Today's devotion concerns what as Christians we

believe about the sinful, fallen state of humanity and how we need to be regenerated by the Holy Spirit. We begin in Genesis 3 with the historical fact (not myth) that mankind did disobey God, which changed everything. The first thing we read is how disobedience distorted Adam and Eve's relationship to God in that "they hid" from Him (3:8). It also distorted Adam and Eve's interpersonal relationship in that they blamed each other (3:12–13). Finally, there were consequences to their disobedience. All creation went from "very good" (Genesis 1:31) to a fallen, corrupted, and condemned state. The consequences of physical and spiritual death, along with pain, suffering, and evil, had gained a foothold and now were corrupting creation. Before you leave chapter three, don't miss the compassion of God (3:21) where He clothed their nakedness.

Our reading in Romans offers us the New Testament condensed version of the same history along with some good news. God through the Spirit, a gift of Jesus Christ, is offering regeneration of what was before the fall: "eternity with God." There is a catch however; in John, Jesus teaches Nicodemus that we must be born again of water (baptism for the forgiveness of sin) and the Spirit (Holy Spirit) to live spiritually. In our final reading, Paul shares this same message of washing and rebirth with the young minister Titus as "excellent and profitable for all."

Early in this study, the process of believing was defined as the mental work required to maintain a belief and how it must be continued or the belief will fade away and become unimportant through doubt, unbelief, or disbelief. We learned that this mental process of believing happens under the guidance of the Holy Spirit. The work starts from the Spirit's conviction as He leads a person to a decision to believe (born again). The belief is strengthened as the person begins collecting Bible-inspired information that supports the belief while rejecting any worldly opposition (all under the guidance of the Spirit). The Spirit then begins to accumulate these different beliefs in our thought process, forming the attitudes that stimulate behavioral changes of regeneration in the person. In the first chapter of Romans, Paul refers to this process as daily renewing the mind in the Scriptures while not conforming to the patterns or teaching of this world. As a disciple, are you renewing your mind daily with the truth of Scripture under the guidance of the Spirit?

Belief and Prayer Journal: Do you believe in Spiritual Regeneration? Have you been regenerated by the washing of the word of God? Do you believe enough to tell others of your rebirth? What is holding you back? Pray about what you believe and what you find difficult to believe. Nicodemus went to Jesus to receive help in overcoming what seemed impossible to believe. We also can be born-again—regenerated by God through the power of the Holy Spirit and the Word.

SANCTIFICATION: THE WORK OF THE SPIRIT

God chose you to be saved through the sanctifying work of the Spirit and through belief in the truth. ...that you might share in the glory of our Lord Jesus Christ.
(2 Thessalonians 2:13-14)

Scripture reading:
2 Thessalonians 2:13–17; John 17:13–26;
1 Thessalonians 4:3–8; 5:12–24
(While reading, watch for anything God is revealing, and record God's revelations and your response in your belief journal.)

Is it your custom to set things aside for special occasions? Statistics tell us that most of us are vigilant and will often set aside money, tools, utensils, and even some of our better articles of clothing for special times. In a biblical context, the concept is called *sanctifying*, and the Scriptures are rich with examples of things, places, and even people being set aside for God's will and purpose. Now, to be sanctified unto God implies that one must separate themselves from all that is sinful, impure, and immoral. This type of sanctifying is biblically defined as holiness. It is the work of the Spirit, whereby the believer is called to become holy as God is holy (1 Peter 1:16). It's a call that would be overwhelming if not for the sanctifying work and help of the Holy Spirit. With that in mind, we turn to our first reading where Paul tells the church that we should be thankful for the Spirit's sanctifying work and help. As church we should also draw encouragement by standing firm in the truth of the Gospel of Christ.

Yesterday, we studied the Holy Spirit's process of regeneration in the life of a believer. Today, we will be looking at what we should believe about the Spirit's continuing work of sanctifying believers through the process of holiness. To grasp the idea of holiness, it may be helpful if we start by considering some of the name attributes of the Spirit as revealed in Scripture. The Old Testament commonly refers to the Holy Spirit as the Spirit, the Spirit of God, or the Spirit of the Lord. As we read, they almost seem interchangeable until we consider that the rabbi taught that the "Spirit of God" was used when God's sovereignty was emphasized and the "Spirit of the Lord" was used to demonstrate God's mercy. The two are often used so close to one another one could easily miss the switch from God's judgment to His mercy. Two examples of this teaching are seen concerning Noah (Genesis 6:11–13) and Abraham (Genesis 22:1–11).

Now, as one begins to read the New Testament, they learn how the Spirit takes on new attributes: the Spirit of Christ, the Spirit of Truth, and the Holy Spirit. Again, there is but "one" Spirit, the same Spirit of the Old Testament but revealed by God to humanity in a fresh new way to make God's will and purpose ever more clear. Thus, the Spirit is revealed as the Spirit of Christ as Savior, the Spirit of Truth as the Word, and the Holy Spirit the maintainer of the Holiness of God. It is also the same Spirit that came at Pentecost to reside in all believers as the Holy Spirit for the purpose of sanctification and holiness.

How important is the Spirit's work of sanctifying? In John, we read that not only did Jesus sanctify Himself, but He prayed that all believers would also sanctify themselves with truth. The same prayer and process are conveyed to the church as the will of God by Paul in our final readings. In them we read of the believer's personal responsibility of obedience to the Holy Spirit's work of sanctification. To make this ever clearer, the Bible warns believers not to resist the Spirit (Acts 7:51), not to grieve the Spirit (Ephesians 4:30–32), not to blaspheme or speak against the Spirit (Matthew 12:31–32), and finally as in our last reading not to quench the Spirit (I Thessalonians 5:19–22).

Belief and Prayer Journal: Are you resisting the sanctifying work of the Spirit in your life? Is there something you are doing or someplace you going that you know would dishonor God? These thoughts and feelings are the Holy Spirit's conviction. The Spirit always has the Lord's mercy for the penitent believer as well as power to aid in helping them to change and move toward God's holiness. Psalm 51 is King David's penitent journal and prayer to God after he sinned. The Spirit wrote it in the Bible because we all, from the greatest to the least of us, will sin. The question is what will you do when you realize it? Psalm 51 is powerful to pray in such times. There is no sin that God can't or won't forgive if we truly repent.

THE HOLY SPIRIT IN THE TRINITY AND IN THE BELIEVER

**On that day, you will realize that I am in my Father,
and you are in me, and I am in you.
(John 14:20)**

Scripture reading:

John 14:1–31; Acts 1:1–11; Acts 2:1–21

(While reading, watch for anything God is revealing, and record God's revelations and your response in your belief journal.)

*T*o *Be Continued* does not make for a good ending. In fact, the mere idea causes us anguish over unresolved thoughts, emotions, and expectations concerning an uncertain future. With that in mind, we can only imagine the thoughts and emotions that Jesus' followers dealt with as they hid out for those fifty days prior to Pentecost. They had followed Jesus for years. Some started as disciples of John the Baptist and then followed Jesus because they understood He was the Messiah. Others were called to follow by Jesus himself, and still others just followed because of the signs, healings, and miracles. More importantly though, all followed for the experience of Jesus' care, protection, teaching, leadership, and counsel. They probably had envisioned themselves as part of some big movement, even to the point of having personal expectations of positions, peace, and grandeur in a new Jewish kingdom. Yet, in the aftermath of Jesus' death, resurrection, and ascension, they all must have been asking: Without Jesus, how can this *continue*? God's answer then, as now, is the Holy Spirit.

Have you ever been privileged to heads-up information on an upcoming change? Now, sometimes as upsetting as change can be, it has a way of encouraging us, especially the spiritual change that Jesus is encouraging in our first reading. You see the disciples knew of the Holy Spirit. The Jewish Scriptures were full of teaching concerning the Spirit of God and how it empowered special events and people like the patriarchs, judges, kings, prophets, and priests of the past to do the will of God. The disciples also knew from John the Baptist that God's Spirit was also empowering Jesus, but as followers they were only common people. Look again at John 14, and note Jesus' teaching on the relationship of intimacy, unity, and oneness between Father, Son, and Holy Spirit in the Godhead of the Trinity. Notice how He portrays it with words like "know," "living in," and "in" (v.9–11). Then note how this same intimate relationship will soon be extended to believers (v.19–20). In verse 17, Jesus explains to the disciples that the Counselor and spiritual Truth that they had *externally with* them (Himself) would in the future be spiritual and *internally in* each and every one of them. The purpose behind this upcoming change of relationship is so that the saving work of God started with Jesus could be *continued* with obedience, love, and witness in them (v.15; 21; 23). It is the same call of discipleship that we experience in our walk of the cross.

In the next two readings in Acts, we read of the fulfillment of Jesus' promises. Read how at Pentecost God poured out His Holy Spirit on all servants, men and women, young and old. In so doing, God sent the gift of relational spiritual empowerment for all believers so as to witness to the saving work of Jesus to a hurting world. We also learned something about God's timing—the prophet Joel foretold this spiritual change some 800 years earlier in his book.

Now, beliefs concerning the Holy Spirit are paramount in and to the Christian Faith and Church. Of these beliefs, none is more important than the Holy Spirit of the Trinity and how it will be in all believers to empower them to *continue* Jesus' mission of reconciling a lost world back to the Father. God's revelation of this Spiritual empowerment is both interpersonal and corporate as church and will be discussed in our later studies on both church and discipleship.

Belief and Prayer Journal: Do you believe in the empowerment of the Triune God (Father, Son, and Holy Spirit)? Pray that your life may reflect and witness to God's Spiritual relationship with and in you. As a believer, have you ever felt the lack of empowerment to continue? Pray to the Spirit of Christ that indwells. Jesus promised to aid us in our struggles and He is our true Spiritual help.

THE HOLY SPIRIT AS A BELIEVER'S COUNSELOR AND EMPOWERMENT

**I will put my laws in their hearts,
and I will write them on their minds.
(Hebrews 10:16)**

Scripture reading:

Hebrews 10:1–25; John 16:5–16; Acts 1:1–11

(While reading, watch for anything God is revealing, and record God's revelations and your response in your belief journal.)

Have you ever worked on one of those "connect the dots" exercises? I'm referring to the ones that start with a page full of seemingly random dots that are numbered. The object of the exercise is to start at dot number one and then draw a line to number two, then on to number three, and so forth. When finished, what seemingly were random dots now become connected in an image. The ancients did a similar thing as they connected certain stars to form constellations in the night sky. The idea is also the source of our common saying: "just connect the dots." We utter it when we would like someone to see the big picture from the small details. Connecting the dots is what Jesus was doing for His disciples in Holy Week and what the Spirit does for us when we read Scripture. The points the Spirit combines are Old Testament prophetic promises with the saving work of Jesus and His teachings of the New Testament. The big picture they become is the Kingdom of God that is empowered by the Holy Spirit and God's will.

Yesterday, we noted Joel's prophecy concerning how God's Spirit will indwell each and every believer as a "Counselor." Now the biblical term Counselor conveys the idea of an advocate knowledgeable in God's Law coming alongside the person as a guide to direct them in legal matters. Connecting that with today's first reading, we see an image resulting from Jesus' perfect sacrifice. It's an image that moves from the "Holy of Holies" in the Jerusalem temple to a personal God who by His Spirit enters into believers to the point of writing His laws on their hearts and minds. In our second reading, Jesus is revealing three points that need to be added concerning what we should believe about the Holy Spirit and His ministry. The first is that the Spirit will convict the "world" of sin, righteousness, and judgment. Jesus uses a legal word "convict" which means to pronounce a guilty verdict which is just, well defined, and exact. This goes beyond just accusing that would allow humanity to justify and rationalize their actions. No, like God's prosecuting attorney, the Spirit brings God's case against all humanity that cannot be excused or evaded. In Jesus' teaching, sin is "unbelief" in both God's messenger and message. Righteousness, on the other hand, is the absolute standard of the Holiness of God by which all the sinfulness of mankind will be judged. Judgment refers to Satan's condemnation and defeat by Jesus' obedience to the Father's will. Satan as the prince of this world is "condemned," again a legal word meaning judged where the sentence is fixed and permanent. The second point or function of the Spirit is to lead disciples into the full understanding of the truth of Jesus' message and teaching as well as to enlighten us concerning future events. Finally, the third function is to glorify Jesus by keeping Him and His message central in a believer's thinking, life, and witness. Now, with a connected image of the work and ministry of the Holy Spirit, we turn to our final reading in Acts. From it we learn that the gift of God's Spirit is the believer's empowerment.

Belief and Prayer Journal: Are you reading and studying Scripture, allowing the Spirit to write on your heart? In your struggle with the sinful nature and unbelief, are you responding to the Spirit's conviction and empowerment? Is your life's focus on the world system or the Truth of God and Christ? Experts tell us that there are two types of witness: what you say and more importantly what you do. Pray and ask God to search your heart so as to convict and empower you to read, study, and believe His Spirit and the Truth of Scripture.

Living by the Spirit and Spiritual Fruit

I am the true vine, and my Father is the gardener. He cuts off every branch that bears no fruit, while every branch that does bear fruit he prunes so that it will be even more fruitful. (John 15:1–2)

Scripture reading:
John 15:1–27; Galatians 5:16–26; Luke 10:1–17
(While reading, watch for anything God is revealing, and record God's revelations and your response in your belief journal.)

If you were to ask a child what their favorite classroom activity was, the answer would most likely be "show and tell." As a teaching method, it most likely finds its origins in the ancient proverb that says: *Tell me and I will forget, show me and I may remember, involve me and*

I will understand. Although not a biblical proverb, its teaching method is found throughout the Scriptures. In fact, scholars believe that most of Jesus' teaching was done by this precise method of involving disciples in their learning process. Such is the case in our first reading. Scholars believe that as Jesus was teaching on "I am the true vine and Spiritual fruit," the disciples were most likely watching, if not laboring, at pruning grapevines. Now, pruning is the essential yearly process of cutting away superfluous and unwanted branches to increase fruitfulness. Jesus knew that in the future, the disciples would have a constant visual reminder of the teaching metaphor. They, as us, would have to remain in a Spiritual relationship of love with the Father through the Spirit of Christ so as to bear "fruit." In the parable, Jesus' teaching moves from "show and tell" to involvement with full knowledge that after His walk of the cross, all relationships would experience a change. Disciples would soon be persecuted and hated by the world system because they were to testify of His saving work done as the Son of God. The love of the Father, mutual love for each other, and obedience to the Counselor (Holy Spirit sent from the Father) would enable them to testify about the truth of Jesus as the Christ. It would be in and through the authority of His name "Jesus" that all disciples would bear spiritual fruit—fruit that will last (v.16).

Israel, being an agriculture-based society, provided for an array of these "show and tell" teachings. The universal experience of growing along with the general knowledge of plowing, sowing, pruning, and harvesting was often effectively used as Bible teaching metaphors. Especially productive is the teaching on living life in the Spirit as in our second reading. In it Paul teaches the church at Galatia with the metaphor of fruit growing. Paul starts with a list of graphic behaviors describing the fruit of a sinful life apart from the Spirit. He warns that those who live this way will not enter the Kingdom of God (heaven). Yet, to those who live their lives by the Spirit of Christ, he offers the promise of the fruit of the Spirit. Note the multiplicity (love, joy, peace, patience, kindness, faithfulness, gentleness, and self-control) but yet it's singularity as fruit growing in the life of the believer. In closing, learning to live a Spirit-led life is a growing process. As disciples, we learn as we read Scripture and allow the Holy Spirit to show (reveal) to us the truth that the Bible teaches. Yet, as our last reading from Luke attests, disciples must involve themselves experientially in the teaching. The Lord desires to send believers as His disciples, trained workers in the name of Jesus, into the harvest field of the world to produce "fruit" that endures in the Kingdom. As disciples, show and tell is our walk of the cross.

Belief and Prayer Journal: Do you get involved with the Bible's teaching? Do you see the list of fruit as your character under growth by the Spirit? Love is given as first priority, with the rest all linked to it and growing out of it. Pray for the Spirit's help to get beyond just the emotionality of love to the true behaviors linked to it through Spiritual fruit.

JESUS' REVELATION OF THE MULTIFUNCTIONAL HOLY SPIRIT

The Counselor (*Paracletos*), the Holy Spirit, whom the Father will send in my name, will teach you all things and will remind you of everything I have said to you.
(John 14:26)

Scripture reading:
John 14:1–31; John 15:26–27; John 16: 7–15; Ephesians 1:11–23;
Acts 1:1–11; Acts 2:1–21
(While reading, watch for anything God is revealing, and record God's revelations and your response in your belief journal.)

Today, as we end the week, we will study the Holy Spirit as *paracletos*, the Greek term Jesus chose to reveal Him as a gift to all believers. The Spirit is a functional gift in that it is important to understand that the *Holy Spirit gave us Jesus and in turn Jesus gives to believers the Holy Spirit.* Therefore, belief in the power and authority of Jesus affords us belief in the power and authority of the Holy Spirit. It is a set of beliefs worth following. Luke tells us that the Holy Spirit "overshadowed" Jesus' mother Mary in the virgin birth of Jesus as Son of God (Luke 1:35). At His baptism, the Holy Spirit descended upon Jesus as a dove (Luke 3:22). From there, the Holy Spirit led Jesus in the wilderness to be tested by Satan (Luke 4:1–2). Luke goes on to tell us that Jesus, after being tested by Satan, was approved by God and began His mission of healing, proclaiming the good news, and seeking and saving the lost. Again, we see that Jesus' entire ministry (miracles, healings, signs, and wonders) were all accomplished by the authority of God and in the power of the Holy Spirit (Luke 4:14; 18–19). It is within this set of beliefs that we as disciples understand what Jesus is implying in our first reading. "Greater things" (v.12), "in my name" (v.13), and "love" and "obedience" (v.15) are how we as believers are to carry on the ministry of Jesus. The passage also teaches the importance of the Holy Spirit and why Jesus used the Greek word "paraclete" to describe His ministry in the lives of believers.

Parakletos is a compound Greek word: *para* meaning alongside, among, beside, or in the sight of, and *kaleo* meaning to call or summon. When you put the two together, you have *parakletos* meaning someone who is called alongside or among others. Now, the question becomes for what purpose. Herein lies the richness of the Greek word along with the variety of the many possible biblical translations into English. Although the NIV prefers Counselor, other translations use one who helps, intercedes, befriends, comforts, or advocates. Thus Jesus is revealing the Holy Spirit as one with both the authority and power of God and who will come alongside believers to counsel, help, intercede, befriend, comfort, and advocate with them in matters of living as a Christian.

We end with Paul's teaching on the Holy Spirit to the saints in the church. In this teaching we learn as believers we are marked with a seal—the promise of the Holy Spirit. The Spirit of wisdom and revelation is given to believers so that we know Jesus even more. In the context of our teaching, Jesus reveals the Spirit and the Spirit reveals Jesus. Keep in mind that revelation in context of Scripture is not intuition or searching of our inner "self." Revelation comes beyond "self." In prayer, it comes when we read and study the Word while we wait and meditate patiently until the answer comes. When it comes, it says "I am the Holy Spirit (parakletos)."

Belief and Prayer Journal: Is your life marked with the seal of the Spirit? Those in doubt should discuss the issue with someone reliable at the church. Keep in mind doubting is a directional focus of choice. It stands in contrast to the direction of believing. Earlier this week, we saw how believers can by unbelief resist, grieve, quench, and even deny the Spirit. Pray to the Spirit for help repenting and believing. Pray with thanksgiving for those Spirit revelations you have experienced.

THE WALK OF THE CROSS
CHRISTIAN DISCIPLESHIP: DYING TO SELF

What the Bible Says We Should Believe
Sunday: a day for contemplation and focused meditation

We've spent this past week looking at what the Bible says we should believe about the Holy Spirit. We started with His work of Regeneration and Sanctification and then moved on to consider the Spirit's divinity and role in the Trinity as well as in the lives of believers. We also considered the many names and titles of the Spirit including the New Testament term "Holy Spirit." From there we considered the Spirit's work in the lives of believers as Spiritual Fruit, and we ended the week with Jesus' revelation of the Spirit as multifaceted, enabling the believer to follow as disciples walking their own walk of the cross. That brings us to the week ahead and what the Bible says we should believe about the church:

Monday: The Church and the Holy Spirit's Gifts
Tuesday: Unity and the Church
Wednesday: Church and the Power of the Gospel
Thursday: Church as a Place for Worship
Friday: Church as a Kingdom of Royal Priests
Saturday: Jesus' Promise to Return for His Church

In the Western tradition, Sunday is called the Lord's day because it is the day Christ was resurrected by God. The Resurrection changed everything in the lives of believers as it provides new life and meaning to come together as a body to fellowship and worship God. Sunday is also our time to review the past week's journal as we contemplate what lies ahead in our study of Jesus' walk of the cross. As was noted earlier, it was a long and arduous journey that took over three years. It began with baptism and testing and from there quickly moved to gathering disciples and choosing apostles as Jesus began traveling about spreading the good news about the Kingdom of God. As His itinerate ministry begins to grow, Jesus starts to send disciples out with the goal of visiting all the towns and villages in Israel and Judah. Last week we focused on those who rejected Jesus as God's Messiah. We learned that some of the Pharisees, Sadducees, teachers of the Law, and even His hometown stumbled over doubt and unbelief. Today we focus on the family of Lazarus and his sisters Mary and Martha. Scriptures tell us that not only did they believe, they also provided hospitality to Jesus on His several visits to Jerusalem including Holy Week (John11:1–12:19; Luke 10:38–41; Mark 14:3–9; Matt. 26:6–13). Read these verses and meditate on how the walk of discipleship is gender-free, with Mary at the feet of the Master and Teacher. Contemplate how her anointing Christ with oil teaches disciples about devotion, compassion, and tenacity as we humble ourselves in our own personal walk to die to self. Meditate also on Martha and her example of discipleship and servanthood as she meets the basic needs of Christ and others. Contemplate her relationship with Jesus as personal to the point that it allowed her the safety to complain and yet confess Him as the Christ, Son of God, the resurrection, and the life. Finally meditate on Lazarus, his friendship with Jesus, his discipleship, his death, and what it meant to be resurrected from death. Contemplate what the Spirit teaches about what we should believe about Jesus as the resurrection and the life in our walk of the cross, dying to self, and discipleship.

THE CHURCH AND THE HOLY SPIRIT'S GIFTS

**Now about spiritual gifts, brothers,
I do not want you to be ignorant.
(1 Corinthians 12:1)**

Start by first reading all of today's scriptures, and while reading attempt to make a composite list of all of the Spirit's gifts.

Scripture reading:
1 Corinthians 12:1–31; 14:12–13; Romans 12:1–13; Ephesians 4:1–13; I Peter 4:7–13
(While reading, watch for anything God is revealing, and record God's revelations and your response in your belief journal.)

We live in a culture that is motivated by the idea of a "free valuable gift." Unfortunately, most of the time what is given as a gift is neither of value nor is it free. This however is not the case with the Holy Spirit and the reasoning for the giving of "spiritual gifts." As for what the Bible teaches on what we should believe, we turn to our first reading. In it Paul challenges the church not to be ignorant. He starts with church dogma and soon changes to the practical usage of spiritual gifts in the church. Likewise, we also will start by first listing the Spirit's gifts: their number, type, and purpose. Then we'll move to how believers and church should discover, utilize, and develop these spiritual gifts. Did you find all nineteen as you read? Now, most experts separate these nineteen gifts into three self-explanatory categories. First are the "Gifts of Speaking": apostolic, prophecy, evangelism, shepherding, teaching, exhortation, knowledge, and wisdom. The second are the "Gifts of Serving": helps, hospitality, giving, government, showing mercy, faith, and discernment. The third and final are the "Gifts to Signify Acts of God": miracles, healings, tongues, and the interpretation of tongues.

As we consider these gifts, it is important to keep in mind several things. The first is purpose. Both Paul and Peter teach "spiritual gifts" are given for the "common good," "building up," "serving," and "edifying" of the church as the body of Christ. It is easy to see their teaching as an extension of Jesus' teaching that "He would build His church" (Matt. 16:18). The second is that it is necessary to differentiate these gifts from one's personal skills, abilities, and talents. This in no way implies that the Spirit won't intensify or heighten a person's talents and skills which in and of themselves come from God. This is about the realization that these gifts provide special spiritual ability and power as they serve the divine purpose of service and ministry as they edify believers. Finally, the gifts of the Spirit are not the fruit of the Spirit we studied last week. They differ in fundamental ways. The first is that gifts are plural and come from without. (This does not imply that all nineteen should be present in every believer; in fact most only receive a few at best.) It is more important to see gifts as a means to an end—spiritually building the church. Fruit, on the other hand, is singular and within, regenerating the person's character back to the image of God, and everyone should possess every variety growing within them. The bottom line is that spiritual gifts are about ministry and service to the church body, whereas fruit is about the Spirit rebuilding a person's character for that ministry and service.

Discovering and developing one's gifts begins with making a personal inventory from the list of nineteen. Outside encouragement from the church is helpful in determining one's gifts. One caution: Although Paul teaches to desire the better gifts, he says discovering one's gifts is to be done by "thinking soberly of oneself" while not quenching the Spirit. As you consider your gift(s), keep in mind the Spirit's goal of building and edifying the church and that all gifts are implements, not ornaments. This is an experiential process of getting involved while learning and developing. Prayer, meditation, and Bible study are necessary components in the understanding of the Spirit's gifts and work in the church.

Belief and Prayer Journal: Small study groups at church on the subject are excellent places to learn, grow, and experience spiritual gifts. They should also be a place of encouragement while developing a gift under the guidance of the Spirit. Keep in mind the Spirit's gifts are for the building up and edifying of the church as a body of believers.

UNITY AND THE CHURCH

**...May they be brought to complete unity to let the world
know that you sent me....
(John 17:23)**

Scripture reading:
Psalm 133; Romans 15:5–7; Colossians 2:2–3; 3:12–14
(While reading, watch for anything God is revealing, and record God's
revelations and your response in your belief journal.)

There was a popular book written a few years ago around the age-old idea that men and women act like they are from different planets. It was one of those self-help books designed to contrast the extreme gender differences between men and women and help them benefit from just understanding the other's perspective as they learned to consider and identify gender differences in styles of thinking and communication patterns. In so doing they were able to correct what was inhibiting the unity in their interpersonal relationship. Oh, if only it was that easy! That brings us to today's study of what the Bible says about relational unity in His church. We start with biblically defining unity as the ability to think and act as one in relationship. It is of extreme importance because the more we are able to come together as couples, people, and church, the less conflict we will have and the easier it will be for God to accomplish His will.

The issue is that we as individuals are always pushing our own agendas, making it difficult to achieve unity, let alone complete unity, especially in church relationships. I say this because Christian unity has purpose that goes beyond just identifying differences of opinion and then compromising. Christian unity in believing families and churches tells a hurting world that God sent His son Jesus to be the peace of the world. So important and purposeful is unity among believers that John records Jesus' prayer in the Garden of Gethsemane for "those who will believe in me." He asked that God would bring all believers—including you and me—into complete unity.

Given our human nature and how different we are in many ways, do you believe it is possible for believers to live in complete unity as church? John Wesley once said, "If your heart is with Christ, give me your hand." This conveys that believers must be unified in believing that Christ is revealed in scriptures as the Son of God and the only way of salvation. With that as our foundation, all other differences lose much of the importance that believers place on them. Today's scriptures tell us that the Spirit of unity is given by God (Romans 15:5) and that being united in love will enable us to know Christ (Colossians 2:2). Is your desire to know Christ so strong that you are willing to allow God to do whatever it takes to unite us in love and make us powerful witnesses to a hurting world?

Belief and Prayer Journal: What do you believe about God's ability to bring unity in your home and in your church, in spite of what may seem to be insurmountable differences? Do you know and believe Him to be "Him who is able to do immeasurably more than all we ask or imagine"? (Ephesians 3:20) Asking God to bring unity in our home and in our church can be a scary request. It may require us to change in ways that may be difficult—to change what we believe. Spend time seeking God's guidance about any areas in your home or church relationships where unity seems to be lacking.

WEEK 5: WEDNESDAY

CHURCH AND THE POWER OF THE GOSPEL

**Whatever happens, conduct yourselves
in a manner worthy of the gospel of Christ.
(Philippians 1:27)**

Scripture reading:
Philippians 1:12–30; 1 Corinthians 15:1–11; 1 Thessalonians 1:1–10
(While reading, watch for anything God is revealing, and record God's
revelations and your response in your belief journal.)

After a lengthy explanation of his involvement in the events, the
child ended by telling his mother: "And that's the Gospel truth!"
"The Gospel truth" is an old idiom that dates back to a time long before
the *Age of Enlightenment*. As an idiom, it is used to provide ethos and
a standard for faith and believing. Unfortunately, as time passes, a

worldly culture is all too willing to replace God's word the Bible as the standard of all truth with the humanism of modern science. For that reason, it is important that as church, believers not only understand the truth and the power of the Gospel of Christ but that we conduct our lives in such a manner to be worthy of that Gospel. In so doing, instead of the worldly culture shaping the church, the church will influence culture with the Gospel of Christ as Paul teaches in our first reading.

Now by definition Gospel literally means to evangelize, tell, or spread "good news." The two terms are often used interchangeably in scripture. To tell someone the Gospel of Christ was in fact to spread the "good news" of Christ and His Kingdom, as in our second reading. In it Paul provides for us a summary of the Gospel's good news of Christ. As believers, we are saved because of Christ's "walk of the cross." That walk involved His suffering, dying, and being buried to pay the price for *our sins*. God raised Him on the third day and provided many appearances of Him alive to serve as witness. As believers and church, our personal witness is when we, like Paul, personalize the Gospel of Christ to "our Gospel" by our "walk of the cross." The telling of "good news" then becomes what Jesus did and is doing in our lives and the life of the church. It is by the power of His Spirit that we also await Christ's glorious return for His church.

At this point in our study, the question becomes more about "how" than "what" or "why" as we turn to our third reading. Here we learn that the Gospel of Christ as shared by Paul, Silas, and Timothy formed the church at Thessalonica. Not only was this church created by the Gospel, but the church worked at spreading the Gospel, and for that, Paul refers to them as both a model church as well as a working church in their culture. In this reading, we also learn that the Gospel shapes the church as the church seeks to live out life according to the Gospel.

This shaping of our lives and church by the power of the Spirit is done through "deep conviction" (vs 5) concerning the Gospel of Christ. Last week in our study of the Holy Spirit, we learned that this "deep conviction" was the work of the Spirit to separate believers from the world and make them holy while regenerating them back to the likeness of Christ. We end with some concluding thoughts on being a model/ working church. It begins with believing and personalizing the Gospel of Christ. Faith in that Gospel then works at shaping our lives and walk as church by the Spirit of Christ. Our love of Christ prompts us to labor at spreading His Gospel. As church we endure in the hope of Christ's return for His church—a model church that is distinguished by faith, love, and hope in the Gospel of Christ. What results is church spreading the good news to the hurting world.

Belief and Prayer Journal: What do you believe about church as an extension of the Gospel? Do you see personalizing and spreading the Gospel of Christ as the Lord's command in Matthew 28:18–20 and Acts 6:7? In the context of this study, could it be said that the church you are attending is both a "model" and a "working" church? Is the Gospel of Christ central in its teachings? Are you and your church fellowship attempting to live life in response to the Gospel of Christ? Journal and pray for insight as well as help to be faithful as church in regard to the Gospel.

Church as a Place for Worship

**God is spirit, and his worshipers
must worship in spirit and in truth.
(John 4:24)**

As you read keep in mind that by the time of Jesus, a great division had arisen between Jews and Samaritans over where and how to worship God. They both had expectations of a coming Messiah, but there was much variance in what that meant.

Scripture reading:
John 4:1–42; 3:1–21
(While reading, watch for anything God is revealing, and record God's revelations and your response in your belief journal.)

Experts tell us that the vast majority of us in our lifetime, because of a multitude of reasons, will find it necessary to change our home church. Any one who has gone through the process knows it is stressful to find a place that meets one's faith and religious needs while also providing a place to belong and worship. As Christians, belonging and participating at a place of worship should be as important as the act of worship itself. Yet, we often overlook God's revelation in Scripture concerning what is truly at the heart of our worship of Him. With that in mind, we turn to our first reading and discover the obvious—"God is spirit" and believers are to worship Him in spirit and in truth. In today's readings, Jesus meets both Nicodemus, a highly respected religious rabbi, and an immoral Samaritan woman right where they are at in life. To both, Jesus offers spiritual truth and insight on the worship of God. The importance of how and where to worship soon gives way to truth—Jesus is their expected Messiah and Christ. He also reveals a new invisible spiritual realm of the kingdom. To enter this spiritual kingdom, one has to repent of sin, "be born again" of God's Holy Spirit, and have a personal encounter with Jesus requiring a worship response. Note the difference: The Samaritan woman is converted and begins to witness to others close to her, whereas Nicodemus quietly fades into his religion only later to timidly defend Jesus in front of the Sanhedrin (John 7:25–44). However, as time passes, Nicodemus will also risk everything as he boldly asks Pilate for the crucified body of Jesus (John 19:38–42). Both Nicodemus and the Samaritan woman came to realize that worship is not about a method or even a place. It is about a relationship with Jesus.

Worship—it must go beyond praising and the ritualistic religious duties of just attending church services. Worship is about paying honor, reverence, thankfulness, and homage to God not just for what

He has done but for who He is. Worship is about surrendering every part of our lives to His control. It becomes "spiritual" when we invite His Holy Spirit to speak to us, to convict us, and to change and comfort us (John 16:5–15). True worship is difficult because it uncovers our sinful self-centeredness as we humbly bow in the presence of a Holy God, desiring to make Jesus the Lord of our lives.

Now, as for the church, nowhere in New Testament scriptures does it designate the church as "the place" for worship replacing the temple, nor is it called a building or an organization. The Bible refers to church as an assembly of believers built into the living body of Christ (1 Cor.12:27). Church is the creation of Christ which He builds (Matt. 16:18), and as members of His body, we are called to both private and corporate worship. Private worship is when we continually pray, read, and meditate on the Word alone or in small groups for personal spiritual maturity. Corporate worship is when we meet as a body under the Lordship of Christ to exercise our spiritual gifts, offer praise and prayers, learn from the Word, and carry out the Father's redemptive mission (Matt. 18:18–20). Church is not just a place for worship, and yet worship should be the highest priority of both the church and the believer. God meant worship to be a lifestyle not just an occasional activity. Jesus said pick up your cross daily and follow (Luke 9:23). Dying to self—this is your daily walk of the cross.

Belief and Prayer Journal: How does this change what you believe about worship? How does it affect your reason for attending church? Which worship do you find easier, individual or corporate? Pray for a thankful heart that can see past race, ethnicity, gender, and class as you worship.

CHURCH AS A KINGDOM OF ROYAL PRIESTS

**But you are a chosen people, a royal priesthood,
a holy nation, a people belonging to God.
(1 Peter 2: 9)**

Scripture reading:
Colossians 2:16–3:4; Revelation 1:1–8, 5:10, 20:6; 1 Peter 2:4–10;
Hebrews 5:1–14; 8:1–6
(While reading, watch for anything God is revealing, and record God's
revelations and your response in your belief journal.)

Have you ever made shadows on the wall for the children? You
know the ones where you position your hands in the light
causing them to cast shadows on the wall that look like various animals. Now, these shadows are not reality, only images that our minds

envision as real. The Bible often uses a similar concept of shadows in its teaching of the truth concerning the New Testament church and worship. In Old Testament Judaism over time, worship became the keeping of a set of rules and regulations set forth by Torah concerning diet, Sabbath, festivals, sacrifice, and the priesthood. In this worship, religious importance was placed on the city of Jerusalem and the temple with its altar and sacred objects. Yet in the New Testament, the Bible refers to these as only shadows on the wall of time—shadows in that they are only shadowy images of a future reality that God would bring about in Christ as the Messiah. In our first reading, Paul is employing this idea of shadows in his teaching to the church at Colosse. The church was in real danger of wanting to hold on to all the shadowy images of Old Testament religious worship. Paul is teaching them that they have a new spiritual freedom from all these rules of worship when they believe in the death and resurrection of Christ. In this spiritual freedom, the church is not subject to false humility and worldly self-imposed worship if they set their minds on things above where Christ is seated.

So with that in mind, we realize that the church is not those shadowy Old Testament images. The question then becomes what is the New Testament church? The answer is found in our next two readings in Revelation and 1 Peter. In them, we read that the church is the body of Christ, and as the church of Christ, we are a chosen people, a royal priesthood, a holy nation (kingdom), and a people belonging to God in Christ. Now for the most part, all of these attributes of being church are self-explanatory. Yet there is one description, "a royal priesthood," that for some may still be cloaked by the shadows of the Old Testament past. So to gain some clarity on what it means to serve God as a "priest" under the authority of Jesus Christ, we move on to our readings in the book of Hebrews. From these two scriptures, we learn that Jesus is our "high priest" and His priesthood is of a "royal" nature because it is based on the Old Testament figure "Melchizedek," the Priest and King of Salem. We also learn some of the duties involved in this priesthood. Firstly, a priest serves as mediator between God and the people as they instruct and teach the people about God. Secondly, as a priest, believers are called to draw near to God on the people's behalf, offering gifts of prayers and intercession. Finally, as church this priesthood is "God calling believers to be in a sanctifying relationship with Christ through the power of the Spirit." In closing, church is a group of chosen sanctified believers called to serve as royal priests belonging to God. One of the more important parts of this priestly duty is to proclaim the Gospel of Jesus Christ to a lost and hurting world.

Belief and Prayer Journal: In Hosea 4:6, the prophet states that both the priest and the people suffer from a lack of knowledge—Scriptural truth. How is your pursuit of knowledge of truth about God? Do you see "teaching" this knowledge contained in the command of Jesus to "make disciples" of the nations (Matt. 28:18–20)? Church attendance is dropping. Pray about your role as a priest, and ask God to reveal to you those needing a mediator to tell them of His love.

JESUS' PROMISE TO RETURN FOR HIS CHURCH

**The Lord is not slow in keeping his promise,
as some understand slowness. He is patient with you,
not wanting anyone to perish,
but everyone to come to repentance.
(2 Peter 3:9)**

Scripture reading:
John 14:1–21; Acts 1:1–11; 1Thesssalonians 4:13–18; 2 Peter 3:1–18
(While reading, watch for anything God is revealing, and record God's revelations and your response in your belief journal.)

Have you ever experienced the comforting and encouraging power of a promise? This power comes from not only "what" is being promised, but from "who" is doing the promising. Never is this truer than when the provider of the promise is God. It captures the old Jewish proverb that says: there is no pillow as soft as God's promise. The proverb conjures up pleasant images of resting our anxious thoughts in and on God's unbreakable promises. With that in mind, we turn to our first reading in John where Jesus is comforting the anxious thoughts of His Disciples. We know this time as the Lord's Last Supper, but to the Disciples, it was a stressful time where Jesus was revealing His mission to and beyond the cross. His followers could scarcely take in the idea of Him going back to the Father. To comfort and encourage them, Jesus reassured them with the promise of His return and the Father's gift of the Holy Spirit to aid them until His return.

Jesus' "promise to return," the Lord's Second Advent, marks a protracted period of time and is often referred to in Scriptures as "the end times," "the last days," or "the day of the Lord." The period contains a multitude of prophetic events: "the end of this Age," "Rapture of the Church," "the Great Tribulation," "Millennium rule of Christ," "Judgment," "punishment of Satan and evil," and "Eternity," just to highlight a few. Now, as for these prophetic events and their associated promises, scholars caution readers to understand them based on *to whom* they are directed. Scholars offer four classifications to help us in our understanding of them. The first is promises and events concerning Jesus as the Messiah, Prophet, Priest, and King; the second is those relating directly to the Nation of Israel; the third is those made concerning the Gentiles; and the fourth is those concerning the Church. Experts also caution readers not to equate Israel with the Church. Therefore, our readings today will focus on what the reader should believe concerning Jesus' promise to return for His Church.

From the Last Supper, we move to Acts where we learn that after Jesus commissioned the Church to baptize, witness, and spread the

Good News, He ascended into heaven on the clouds. We also learn that He will come again in the same way. In 1 Thessalonians we learn how believers will be caught up in the clouds to be with the Lord at the angel's trumpet call. Scholars refer to this as the Rapture of the Church, the end of this age, and the beginning of the Tribulation. That leaves us with the timing. Scriptures tell believers to be always ready because no one knows the day and hour, and yet, as time passes, some tend to doubt and disbelieve, which brings us to the reading in 2 Peter. There we learn that the Lord is not slow in time but patient with the desire that everyone might come to salvation. Peter encourages as he reframes our doubt and disbelief by asking us to recall all the promises God has previously kept. He then has us separate worldly thoughts and ideas from the spiritual, including the concept of time. Peter ends by linking readers into the Lord's mission. He tells them to be forward-looking people living blameless lives at peace with God while growing in grace and knowledge of the Lord as an example to those unsaved.

Belief and Prayer Journal: Are you resting on God's promises and growing in knowledge of Scripture? Does doubt cloud your readiness to those around you? Ask the Spirit's Help.

THE WALK OF THE CROSS
CHRISTIAN DISCIPLESHIP: DYING TO SELF

What the Bible Says We Should Believe
Sunday: a day for contemplation and focused meditation

We've spent this past week looking at what the Bible says we should believe about being church. We started with gifts of the Spirit for the purpose of building the church body. Then we looked at the importance of unity in the body in conjunction with the will of God. Midweek we looked at the power of the Gospel as the good news, advancing the church and enticing a hurting world to come to salvation and healing. We ended the week with what the Bible says we should believe about our role as royal priests in church and Jesus' promise to return for His church. That brings us to the week ahead and what the Bible says we should believe about the Scriptures themselves:

Monday: Vows, Oaths, and Promises
Tuesday: The Scriptures (Bible) as Truth
Wednesday: The Bible as God-Breathed
Thursday: Metaphor and the Bible
Friday: The Bible: Prophecy and Discernment
Saturday: The Bible and Revelation

Sabbath (Christian Sunday) in Hebrew literally means "to cease" or "rest." It is the day God rested from His creation work. God also set the day aside as a day for humanity to rest and focus on things of eternal importance and spiritual growth. The Bible tells us that it was Jesus' custom to attend synagogue on the Sabbath (Luke 4:16). Now, synagogue means house of assembly and is the Jewish equivalent of church. It was and is their center of the religious community and a place for prayer, study, and education, as well as social and charitable work. As we review and contemplate Jesus' walk of the cross, Sabbath and synagogue play an important role. They served not only as a place for Jesus' teaching and preaching but also God's revelation and activity through several accounts of healings, restoration of sight, and the casting out of demons. As in the past weeks, we saw that there were those who rejected Him as their Messiah and there were those who opened their homes, hearts, and synagogues. As the destination of the cross looms ever closer, the training of the disciples becomes more of Jesus' focus. Today we meditate on two interconnected sets of Scriptures concerning the training of the disciples. The first is Jesus' teaching that as the Messiah, He must be rejected, suffer, and die after which in three days He will rise (resurrection) (Matt. 16:13–26; Mark 8:27–37; Luke 9:18–25). The teaching starts with the question, "who do people say I am?" After the disciples stumble through some answers, Jesus then asks, "who do you say I am?" to which Peter confesses He is the son of God. The second set of Scriptures deals with Jesus and His transfiguration as a display of both His divinity and glory as attested by the voice of God (Matt. 17:1–13; Mark 9:2–13; Luke 9:28–36).

Meditate on these scriptures and then contemplate first how you would answer the question "who do you say I am?" Then move on to Jesus' transfiguration. Contemplate how encouraging this must have been for Jesus to meet with Moses and Elijah on His way to the cross. Contemplate also the connection between suffering and glory and the impact on the disciples to see the Lord in this new way.

VOWS, OATHS, AND PROMISES

**Simply let your 'Yes' be 'Yes,' and your 'No,' 'No';
anything beyond this comes from the evil one.
(Matthew 5:37)**

Scripture reading:
Matthew 5:33–37; 23:16–22; Deuteronomy 6:13; 23:21–23;
Ecclesiastes 5:4–6; Numbers 30:1–16; James 5:10–19
(While reading, watch for anything God is revealing, and record God's
revelations and your response in your belief journal.)

Last week we looked at the comfort found in Jesus' promise to return for His church. However, today the focus shifts to how we as people make promises, along with vows and oaths to offer others comfort and assurances. During each of our lives, most of us will make promises to our children, vows to spouses, and even at times swear legal oaths. Each of these will play a huge part in defining who we are as a nation, church, and people of faith. Each should also be greatly influenced by what we believe about God and the Bible. After all, is it not the Bible we place our hand on for an oath, and are not our promises and vows pledged in the name of God and to God? To that we need to add Jesus' cautionary teachings in our first readings along with some basic biblical definitions and Old Testament reasoning. A *promise* is a verbal or written agreement to either do or not do something, whereas an *oath* is an appeal to God to witness the truth of a promise made. This brings us to a *vow*, which is a voluntary promise made to God to perform some service or abstain from doing something in return for some hoped-for benefit. Finally, to *pledge or swear* is to offer something as security until the oath or vow is completed.

As history goes, ancient peoples were highly superstitious and often used the name of a specific god to validate what was said. This made the making of vows and oaths a common feature in helping someone persuade another that what they were saying was truth. Because oaths and vows involved various false gods, not only was the process abused to hide a lie, it also distorted the people's religious expression and worship. These historic facts present a problem in both Judaism and Christianity because the Lord our God is one, He is Holy, He is jealous, and He is deeply concerned with the sacredness and usage of His name (third Commandment Ex. 20:7). By the time of Jesus, the scribes and teachers of the Law had the art of oath and vow making down to a science by providing a way out. They did this by getting people to change from the name of God to a list of sacred things, thus nullifying what was said. It was from this context that Jesus taught about the importance of all that comes out of our mouths (Matt. 15:11).

Now, it is not that Jesus or the Bible is forbidding the making of promises, oaths, and vows because in fact they do play a big part in our culture and religious experience. What is being taught is the sacredness and accountability that are expected from believers in honoring what they say. They are sacred because Scripture teaches that when they are made, they are only to be uttered in the name of God. They require accountability because they are strictly voluntary and as such come with an obligation to be fulfilled in a timely manner. In our final reading on this subject, James cautions us to use patience when faced with trials, persecutions, and trouble instead of swearing vows and oaths. Like Jesus, his teaching is also to let your yes be yes and your no be no.

Belief and Prayer Journal: Most homes have several Bibles lying out for all to see. To some they are only amulets warding off evil as the ancients did, and to others they are read, studied, and valued as the word of God. How do you use and value the Bible? I swear to God, God only knows, and it's God's truth are but a few of the casual vows misusing God's name. Pray for the Spirit's help in considering your casual usage of vows, oaths, and promises.

The Scriptures (Bible) as Truth

**If you hold to my teaching,
you are really my disciples. Then you will know the truth,
and the truth will set you free.
(John 8:31–32)**

Scripture reading:
John 8:12–47; John 18:28–19:16; Luke 24:13–49
(While reading, watch for anything God is revealing, and record God's
revelations and your response in your belief journal.)

Yesterday we learned that when we take oaths sworn on the Bible
and in the presence of God, we are stating the truth of a situation
as we experienced it. However, our world is full of situations which
go beyond the truth of our understanding: war, poverty, sickness,

disease, evil, and social injustice. As a believer and a disciple, where do you go to find the truth, the whole truth, and nothing but the truth of what is happening around you? Is your source the worldly nightly news or maybe you turn to some known Christian news--based source? (Unfortunately both are subject to human bias with an agenda.) Today, we are looking at what we should believe about the Scriptures as the believer's source for the Truth. St. Augustine once said about the Bible: "The truth is like a Lion. You don't have to defend it. Let it loose. It will defend itself." As a disciple, have you let the Bible loose in your life? Has Jesus' teaching set you free as He has promised, or are you like those in our first reading who are stuck in their sin and worldly traditions? As often in Jesus' teachings, He clearly states the obvious: "He who belongs to God hears what God says" (vs.47). Previously in this study, we learned that the Holy Spirit as our Counselor takes the word of God when we read it and writes it on our hearts resulting in both our hearing and belonging to God (John 16:13; Heb. 10:16). In this first reading, Jesus is teaching us that as a believer, we are free from being a slave to the curse of sin and death in this world system. Believers now have a permanent place in the Family of God (vs.36), a truth that is contrary to the secular news of the world.

The Bible is rich with examples of those who fail to understand Scripture as truth. With that we move to our second scripture on truth. In it we read about one of the saddest dramas in the Bible, when Pilate asked Jesus "what is truth?" and then leaves the room before getting an answer. Truth was standing right in front of him, but Pilate, like a lot of people, had his eye on the worldly circumstance at hand and not on God. Pilate's agenda was to please everyone while advancing his own career by keeping peace between the Roman and Jewish worlds.

Unfortunately, Pilate missed an opportunity to hear the truth of the prophetic drama of redemption which was playing out around all of them. Now, it is inappropriate for the reader to speculate a different outcome for Pilate, Caiaphas, the Jews, or even the world order. To do so would be to miss John's teaching concerning the Gospel of Jesus and His walk of the cross along with the glory of resurrection and redemption as the fulfillment of the truth.

In the drama of Holy Week it seems Pilate, along with the Jews and the Romans, was not the only one avoiding the truth of Old Testament prophetic Scriptures. In our final reading, we learn that two of Jesus' own disciples were confused and bewildered and leave town for Emmaus. Despite the news of the resurrection, these two were "downcast"—*their expectation* (agenda) of Messiah had been crushed, so they're heading off dejected and unable even to recognize Jesus. As you read, imagine what it would have been like to walk along with them and hear Jesus open the truth of the Old Testament as it related to Messiah and the redemption drama. As you read on in Luke's Gospel account, do not miss the phrase "everything must be fulfilled that is written in the Scriptures." It is a unique biblical phrase used over forty times in the New Testament alone to refocus believers from worldly agendas to the truth of scripture. In ending, biblical truth is like a lion. Let it loose in your life, and, with the Spirit's help, read it, study it, believe it, and apply it to all the situations of life and you will be free indeed as you walk in the Truth of your own walk of the cross.

Belief and Prayer Journal: Have you ever found yourself bewildered and confused like the two on the road to Emmaus? James 1:5 offers assurance that the truth will be given generously to those who ask God. Journal today about how the New Testament is a living journal of

God's truth from ages past and suitable for your life's situations today. Pray to the Spirit for help, strengthening your beliefs about the Bible as God's truth. Pray also for help to walk in that Truth on your personal walk of the cross as you continue to die to self.

THE BIBLE AS "GOD-BREATHED"

**All Scripture is God-breathed and is useful for teaching,
rebuking, correcting and training in righteousness,
so that the man of God may be thoroughly equipped for
every good work.
(2 Timothy 3:16–17)**

Scripture reading:
2 Timothy 3:1–17; Genesis 2:7; Job 4:9; Psalm 18:15; John 3:1–8;
20:22; Acts 2:1–4; Revelation 11:11–12
(While reading, watch for anything God is revealing, and record God's
revelations and your response in your belief journal.)

Don't you just love a good idiom? Today's is *don't waste your
breath*. It's employed by someone who has made up their mind
and wants to stifle anyone trying to influence them differently. As
an idiom it is used to reference a "closed-minded person." In the

context of the Christian Faith, a "closed-minded person" is one who is worldly and blinded to the influence of the Spiritual truth of Scripture, whereas an "open-minded person" is influenced by the Bible because it is God-breathed and profitable to teach, convince, correct, and train the believer in the ways of God. With that we turn to our opening Scripture, where the imprisoned Paul writes to the young and upcoming Timothy who will carry on for him. Paul, never one to sugarcoat his words, tells Timothy to take caution because there will be terrible times ahead where people will love themselves and deny God's power. Paul reminds Timothy of his "way of life" and his "teaching" and tells him that he too should live the same life of service. Paul continues by telling Timothy that he also must endure sufferings and persecutions but he should have faith because the Lord will rescue. After all this caution, Paul finally encourages and directs with that great little phrase "but as for you." Timothy, as well as all believers, will be different because he reads, studies, and believes the Holy Scriptures. Paul reminds us that the Bible is God-breathed and has the power to make us wise for salvation through what we believe about Christ Jesus as we ground our faith in Him.

Paul claims the Scriptures have power because they are *God-breathed—(theopneustos)*. It is a term he coined and only uses in 2nd Timothy to go beyond saying divinely inspired. Paul compounded the Greek *theo* meaning God and *pneu-stos* meaning "breathe out" to convey a deeper meaning. *Pneu-stos* stems from the word *pneuma* meaning "wind, air, breath, or spirit" as an invisible force capable of mysterious work. It captures the biblical idea that breath, spirit, and spiritual soul all have the properties of wind. Paul's bottom line is that God-breathed Scriptures were written under the invisible spiritual force of God and have the mysterious power to sanctify believers as they teach, convince, correct, and train.

Although the term "God-breathed" was coined by Paul, it was not a new idea and can be traced as a thread throughout the tapestry of scriptures. We start in Genesis with man being made out of dust into which God breathed the "breath of life" or his soul. Next, we go to Job and Psalms where we learn that it is the same "breath of God" that destroys all that is evil. In the Gospels, Jesus explains to Nicodemus that all believers wanting to enter the kingdom of God must be "born again" by that same "Spirit of God." Later in John, the risen Jesus will "breathe" temporary spiritual help on His disciples as they wait for Pentecost. In Acts, we see the birth of church (Pentecost) out of a "heavenly wind" as tongues of fire anoint believers with the "Holy Spirit." Finally that thread ends in the last days of Revelation with that same "breath of life" from God resurrecting the "two faithful witnesses" who lay dead in the street for three days. In closing when it comes to the "breath of God" and the Bible as "God-breathed," are you open or closed minded?

Belief and Prayer Journal: What do you believe about the power of God's word the Bible? Are you allowing it to teach, convince, correct, and train you in the ways of God? How about as an aid in witnessing? Pray, thanking the Holy Spirit for God's insight available to all believers.

METAPHOR AND THE BIBLE

Your word is a lamp to my feet and a light for my path.
(Psalm 119: 105)

Scripture reading:

Psalm 119:105-112, 129-136; 2 Peter 1:19-21 (Light); Psalm 19:7-11; I Corinthians 3:1-3; 1 Peter 2:1-6; Hebrews 5:7-14 (Food); Ephesians 5:21-33; James 1:19-27 (Appearances); Ephesians 6:17; Hebrews 4:12 (A sword for spiritual battle); Mark 4:1-20; 1 Peter 1:23 (Seed for sowing) (While reading, watch for anything God is revealing, and record God's revelations and your response in your belief journal.)

Have you ever wondered why a picture is worth a thousand words? Researchers have long shown that our brains use pictures as part of the human thinking process. That is the reason it is often said "picture this in your mind." These pictures gain power when constructed with powerful imagery and symbolism such as Jesus as a *lamb* and Spirit as a *dove*. They gain power because they have the ability to stimulate strong emotions in us and our thinking process. Now, our thinking process takes on an additional richness when we expand it with the use of metaphors. This happens when we allow our brains to apply the imagery, symbolism and attached emotions of one thing to something which is not intended, as in our opening scripture. It is a perfect example of the many metaphors the Bible uses to help believers assimilate the word of God into their thinking. Today we will consider a few of these powerful metaphors in God's Scriptures.

Turn back to our first reading from Psalm 119, a long acrostic poem written to the glory of God and His word. In it the Psalmist describes God's word as "light from a lamp" shining in the darkest of times for the believer. Peter in his epistle captures this same idea, only he has God's word shining into the dark places of our heart to bring about change. From there we continue with God's word as "food," where now the Psalmist not only compares God's word to honey but claims it to be more valuable that gold. In our next readings, we have Paul, Peter, and the writer of Hebrews comparing Scripture to both milk and solid food. All three employ this food metaphoric wordplay to establish God's word as necessary substance for growth and maturity (physically and spiritually). From there we move to appearances. As people, most of us are conscious of our dress and cleanliness. This provides the books of Ephesians and James the opportunity to teach via wordplay metaphors. In Ephesians Paul alludes to Scripture as water for washing. Beginning with the believer's baptism into the church, the Scriptures as water should be continually used for cleansing us from all unrighteous. James considers Scripture a mirror into which believers can look to see their true condition. James goes on to teach that we must not turn away forgetting what was revealed but allow the word to change us. Along with the need for a good appearance, the human psyche also has a need for safety and protection. In our next Scriptures, Paul and the writer of Hebrews metaphorically use the word of God as a sharp double-edge sword along with a shield and a helmet to aid the believer in their spiritual battles. Next, we look at the metaphor of God's word as a seed for sowing. This was one of Jesus' favorites which He used many times in various parables of the Gospels. As you read Mark's telling of Jesus' parable, don't get lost in the types of dirt and miss the metaphor of God's word as a seed which needs to be planted in order to grow. In this teaching metaphor is the fact that the word must be planted in our minds through belief and then the believer can plant it in others through witnessing. We end in 1 Peter, where Peter considers God's word with the metaphor of an "imperishable seed" responsible for bringing about rebirth and spiritual growth in all who believe.

Belief and Prayer Journal: Which of today's metaphors in Scripture is drawing you inward? Reread it and meditate on it. Does it conflict with or compliment what you believe? Take time and journal what you hear from the Spirit. Pray about how, as a born-again believer, you can be a sower of the word in others.

THE BIBLE: PROPHECY AND DISCERNMENT

**But everyone who prophesies speaks to men for their strengthening, encouragement and comfort.
(I Corinthians 14:3)**

Scripture reading:
I Corinthians 12:1–11; 14:1–12; Deuteronomy 18:17–22; Isaiah 30:9–10; Acts 3:17–26; I John 4:1–15; Colossians 3:1–17
(While reading, watch for anything God is revealing, and record God's revelations and your response in your belief journal.)

As a believer have you ever considered yourself a prophet of God? As you think about your answer, consider the following. The Bible teaches that a *prophet* is one who is in a personal relationship with God to the point that God can communicate to them via the Holy

Spirit His deepest love and concerns for His people (1 Samuel 3). Jesus taught that being a prophet may not always be popular work, especially in one's hometown (church) where friends and family know you best (Mark 6:4). Finally, consider what Paul teaches in our opening reading. Prophesying, the work of a prophet is a gift of the Spirit that all believers should "eagerly desire." In this teaching Paul also settles a church controversy over the fact that the Spirit's gift of prophecy is more needed than the Spirit's gift of tongues because prophecy builds the church body by strengthening, encouraging, and comforting other believers. Don't miss the fact that Paul also teaches that the Spiritual gift of prophecy should be balanced with the gift of discernment and should be performed with grace and in love. At this point let us revisit the opening question and ask again, as a believer how can you *not* consider yourself a prophet of God?

Today we will look at this relational role of God's prophet/prophetess and the importance of insuring that all prophecy is from God and grounded in scripture as the word of God (discernment). We begin with our readings in the Old Testament and Acts where we learn that the role of prophet was established by God for the intent purpose of communicating His will to His people. Several things can be learned from these readings. The first is that it is God speaking to His people through the prophet by putting His Spirit upon the prophet and His words in their mouth. The second is that the prophetic utterances of the prophet were not just for the benefit of fortune-telling a good future, but *predictive* based on the people's present condition of sinful disobedience. Finally, the relationship between God and the prophet was based on holiness and what they professed was always centered on God's redemptive work through Jesus and a future kingdom. Also, at the heart of this relationship role is the work of the Holy

Spirit (sanctification and regeneration). Now, as we move from the Old Testament into the New Testament, the role of a prophet remains the same. However, the number of those who were called and anointed does change. In the Old Testament, only a select few were anointed with the Holy Spirit and called into this relationship, but at Pentecost and the birth of the New Testament church, all believers are anointed and called (Acts 2).

This brings us to the believer's need to rely on the Spirit's gift of discernment and the study of the Word. Now discernment is often defined as the ability to think both biblically and spiritually, knowing right from wrong and Truth from error. As for spiritually, John in his teachings cautions the believer to "test the spirits" so as to recognize and listen only to the Spirit of Truth from God so that all we do or say is out of love for one another. In our final reading to the church at Colosse, Paul teaches that as God's chosen people, we must set our hearts on things above and let the word of Christ richly indwell us as we teach and admonish each other in love. This requires the believer to read, study, and believe the Bible as the word of God. One final thought—prophecy should always be positively done with healing, love, and grace and never be judgmental. Jesus taught that believers should not judge lest they be judged.

Belief and Prayer Journal: Have you ever been encouraged, strengthened, or comforted by another believer? Journal about what that meant to you. Did you recognize it as God speaking to you through another believer? Pray for discernment and a readiness to speak to other believers.

THE BIBLE AND REVELATION

**I keep asking that the God of our Lord Jesus Christ,
the glorious Father, may give you the Spirit of wisdom and
revelation, so that you may know him better.
(Ephesians 1:17)**

Scripture reading:
Ephesians 1:3–23; 1 Corinthians 2:6–16; Romans 16:25–27
(While reading, watch for anything God is revealing, and record God's
revelations and your response in your belief journal.)

D o you know the difference between knowledge and wisdom?
How about insight and revelation? As pairs they sound like
synonyms of each other, but they are not. *Knowledge* is when we collect facts and accumulate data via our senses, whereas *wisdom* is the
ability to process those facts and make wise judgments based on their
deeper meaning. *Insight* is when one thinks they truly know the deeper

meaning and true nature of things stemming from the processing of their gathered knowledge. *Revelation* on the other hand is when the nature and true meaning of things are revealed to someone externally from their thought process. I review this because knowing the meaning of wisdom and revelation is central in the study of God and the Bible. As believers we don't discover the deeper meaning of things by searching the Scriptures, nor is it possible for anyone to know the mind of God. Yet God, through the Bible, self-reveals Himself so that people might know, love, trust, serve, and obey Him as their Lord and God. This week we have been looking at what we should believe about the Bible and its Spirit-imparted wisdom. Today we will close the week with the Bible as God's self-revelation of His own divine nature, will, and character where believers gain wisdom as they come to know Him better.

With that in mind, we turn to our first reading. In it Paul is praising God for all the Spirit's blessings given to us through Christ including wisdom and understanding of the mystery of God's will. Paul's use of the word *mystery* carries the connotation that the true meaning and nature of God and His will was unknowable and kept secret until God chose to reveal it in Christ. Also note Paul's use of relationship words such as love, forgive, grace, chosen, adoption, inheritance, and to-know (intimacy). Paul's prayer is not for believers to have knowledge and insight but to experience God and Christ through the wisdom of Scripture where God's Spirit reveals Himself by calling believers to a unique personal relationship and church. For more on the uniqueness of this personal relationship and the mystery concerning God and His will, we turn to our next reading from Paul to the church at Corinth. In this reading Paul differentiates God's hidden secret wisdom from worldly knowledge and insight. Paul explains in great detail how God's wisdom is revealed only to believers because they have God's Spirit and the mind of Christ. Having the mind of Christ allows the Spirit to teach believers concerning the deeper meaning of things while revealing God's true nature and will. The Spirit's teaching is in fact wisdom that when compared to the world's wisdom will sound foolish. We end with our final reading where Paul again shares this same teaching on the Spirit's revelation, mystery, and wisdom from God, only this time to the church at Rome. It is part of Paul's personal Gospel of good news to the church, and it is wisdom that was made known through the prophetic writings (Scripture) by the command of God.

In closing, the Bible is more than just a book to believers. It is a library of sixty-six books where God chose to self-reveal His own divine nature, will, and character. It is sacred writings where we as believers can read under the teaching of the Spirit and gain wisdom while coming to know Him better as Father, Son, and Spirit.

Belief and Prayer Journal: Surveys show a decreasing trend of the Bible being read from the pulpit and in the homes, yet it is the place to know God (Father, Son, and Spirit). At the heart of this trend is a problem of belief in Scripture. All beliefs grow out of a *decision* to believe. Have you made a decision on God's self-revelation the Bible? Join Paul in his prayer to God for the Spirit of wisdom and revelation.

THE WALK OF THE CROSS
CHRISTIAN DISCIPLESHIP: DYING TO SELF

What the Bible Says We Should Believe
Palm Sunday: a day for contemplation and focused meditation

We've spent this past week looking at what the Bible says we should believe about the Scriptures themselves. We began with the importance of keeping our vows, oaths, and promises and then we looked at Scripture as Truth. Midweek we considered what is meant by saying the Word is God-breathed. Next, we looked at the Bible's usage of metaphors and its connection with prophecy and discernment. Finally, we learned that the Word is God's self-revelation of His true character to those who read it. That brings us to the week ahead and what the Bible says we should believe about discipleship:

Monday: Calling of Believers to Discipleship
Tuesday: Knowing God: Intimacy with Jesus
Wednesday: Discipleship and Belonging to God
Maundy Thursday: Discipleship and Prayer
Good Friday: Discipleship: The Walk of the Cross as Dying to Self
Saturday: Discipleship and the Ministry of Reconciliation

Our worship today marks the start of Holy Week. It begins with Palm/Passion Sunday, the day Christ the King made His triumphal ride on a donkey down the Mount of Olives into Jerusalem fulfilling the prophecies of Isaiah 62:11 and Zechariah 9:9. It is called Palm because as the procession went along, the people celebrated by laying palm branches on the route to honor Him. It is called Passion because as He approached, He passionately wept over Jerusalem and its rejection of Him. This is the last week of His earthly ministry and teaching on the coming Kingdom of God. The first part of the week, He will cleanse the temple, teach, and denounce the scribes and Pharisees along with their pseudo-religious teaching. On Tuesday afternoon He will ascend the Mount of Olives with His disciples and prophetically warn them of things to come. As they gaze at the beauty of the Temple and Jerusalem He will foretell of its future destruction and how, as His disciples, they will suffer persecution and tribulations. Nightly, He will return to Bethany where Mary will anoint Him and many will come to be with Him. Wednesday is believed to be the day Judas will conspire with the temple Priests and officials to betray Jesus for thirty pieces of silver. On Maundy Thursday, as the Jewish Passover approaches, He will instruct His disciples to go and prepare the Passover meal in an upper room in the lower part of Jerusalem for them to celebrate together that night. It is called Maundy, meaning commandment, because during this

Last Supper, Jesus gave the disciples a new commandment—to love one another (John 13:4). He also demonstrated this love of a servant by washing their feet and establishing God's new covenant with the sacraments of His blood (wine) and body (bread) as a testament to remember, after which they move to the Garden of Gethsemane and His prayerful agony. By 2 AM he is betrayed, arrested, and falsely tried by Ananias, Caiaphas, Herod, and Pilate. He will be denied, mocked, thorn-crowned, beaten, and by 9:00 AM Good Friday morning will be crucified. After the agony of the cross, He will utter "it is finished" and by 3:00 PM in the afternoon be dead and moved to the tomb. As for Good, there are a multitude of reasons, most of which center around Jesus' sacrifice of salvation being good for believers. After three days and what appears to be great loss, Jesus rises from the grave on Easter or Resurrection Sunday "passing over" from Old Testament to New Testament, connecting the two. Over the next forty days, many will witness and give testimony of the risen Christ, but none more important than the last on the mountain in Galilee. Today's subject for meditation and contemplation is Matthew 28:16–20, the Great Commission. Jesus gives final instruction to spread His teaching to all nations. As a disciple, contemplate the great cost of salvation and discipleship and how you are personally connected to its progression in your personal walk of the cross as the Spirit aids in your dying to self.

THE CALLING OF BELIEVERS TO DISCIPLESHIP

**Therefore my brothers, be all the more eager to
make your calling and election sure.
(2 Peter 1:10)**

Scripture reading:
2 Peter 1:1–15; Psalm 116; Ephesians 1:11–19a; Matthew 28:19-20
(While reading, watch for anything God is revealing, and record God's
revelations and your response in your belief journal.)

As a Christian, how would you tell someone about discipleship?
Does your understanding go beyond just going to church and
following Jesus? Would you focus on the emotionality of an intimate
spiritual relationship with the Lord and how it is not only empowering
but uniquely personal to each believer? Maybe you would focus on

the relational responsibility stemming from His divine grace and love, emphasizing it is a responsibility that invites an active response from believers to witness, grow in self-control, and produce fruit as they identify (be yoked) with the passion and suffering of Christ. Maybe you might go as far as to tell them that discipleship is the answer to all those who ask, "God what is your will for my life?"

Our understanding of Christian discipleship is central to the faith. For that reason, we will spend the week looking at what the Bible says we should believe about it as a personal relationship with Jesus. What better place to start than with His calling and election? Now, the Bible uses the word "call" in several unique ways. The first is calling or descriptively naming something. In Genesis 2:23 Adam called Eve "woman" because she was taken out of man, and in Acts 11:26 we read that believers were first called Christians (followers of Christ) at Antioch. The second way the Bible uses "call" is to identify a person's vocation. St. Matthew was called a tax collector and Jesus was called rabbi (teacher). Finally, the word call is used as an invitation to a personal relationship. In 1 Corinthians 1:9 we read that God has called us into fellowship with Jesus and we can expect God to be faithful to that call.

There are a couple things to keep in mind concerning the call of God into relational fellowship. First, the call comes with total freedom on our part to choose not to respond. Second, the relationship is bi-directional. As Christians, we are invited to call on the name of the Lord in both good and bad times (Psalm 116). In Romans 12:13, Paul says that all who believe and call on the name of the Lord will be saved. What we believe about this call of God in and on our lives is important. Not only does it serve as the foundation for a personal relationship with God, but it also begins our process of salvation. The surety of our calling and election is so important that the aged Peter wanted to remind us again and again of the importance to make it sure. To make it sure means to make it real. Peter provides us with seven increasing measures based on Jesus' teaching that we need to add to our faith: goodness, self-control, perseverance, godliness, brotherly kindness, and love, all of which make for a sure faith.

Belief and Prayer Journal: As a Christian, what do you believe about the call of God in and on your life? How would you tell someone about the tough stuff—the responsibilities that come with His calling? Look at the seven measures given by Peter. Which is your weakness and which is your strength? Ask God's help for the weakness and praise Him for your strength. Christ was ever aware of God's call to the cross for our salvation. Holy week culminates Christ's Lenten journey and the responsibility that the Father set before Him. Ask the Holy Spirit to refresh and remind you of your call to be in fellowship with Christ, especially His passion for others.

KNOWING GOD:
INTIMACY WITH JESUS

**"Who are you, Lord?" Saul asked. "I am Jesus,
whom you are persecuting," he replied.
(Acts 9:5)**

Scripture reading:
Acts 9:1–31; Acts 22:1–21; Acts 26; Matthew 28:16-20
(While reading, watch for anything God is revealing, and record God's
revelations and your response in your belief journal.)

It is said that if you are asking the wrong questions, you're getting
the wrong answers. The issue here is that along with those wrong
answers comes wrong thinking and wrong conclusions. Now, this
distorted questioning process could never be more problematic than
when we are seeking to know the Lord in our walk of the cross as

disciples. It is problematic because of the fact we are asking questions of an infinite and Spirit God (John 4:24).

As humans we are unique in all creation in that we have the ability to communicate with each other via language. It is through language's mutual process of questioning that we can know each other personally and intimately. As Christians our faith is unique in that we believe that God broke into history (Jesus' incarnation) to be personally related to believers and be intimately known through the process of questioning and discipleship. The idea of intimacy as God wanting us to know Him and be known by Him is a theme that runs throughout the Bible. God not only searches our hearts, but He encourages His people to share their deepest thoughts, emotions, and needs in prayer through Jesus name. The uniqueness of the New Testament is that all believers are filled with the Holy Spirit so that even in our weakness, the Spirit intercedes for the people of God in accordance with God's will (Romans 8:26–28). Yesterday we learned that Christian discipleship is a relationship that begins with a believer's response to God's call and election on their life. Today we are looking at how a believer should respond to that call. What better biblical example than Saul's call and conversion in our first reading? Note Saul's first question to Jesus: Who are you Lord? This is the first question to ask when meeting the Lord because it invites the Lord to reveal His true identity, personality, and will. It is through the "who are you" question that we like Saul gain the experience of knowing Him intimately and personally as Father, Savior, and Holy Spirit.

Now, it is not that other questions such as those beginning with the words why, how, what, where, and when are wrong. They would only be out of sequence as they would prematurely lead the believer into Christ's work (salvation, redemption, and justification) without first experiencing the uniqueness of a personal relationship. More simply, one would know about God (be religious) without knowing God through an intimate relationship with Jesus. Also these other questions take the focus away from repentance as they reinforce our human importance, pride, and self-centeredness in the relationship. As you read, note the obedience of both Paul and Ananias to the Lord's will for Paul to suffer for the name of Jesus through being an apostle to the Gentiles, Kings, and Israel. Through his obedience Paul receives his sight back, is filled with the Spirit, and becomes an active part in the process of church and discipleship. As you read the other readings in Acts, note how Paul retells this conversion experience as a witness to those Jews, Gentiles, and Kings as he makes his way to Rome and his death. Obedient discipleship enabled Paul to be used in a powerful way by the Lord, making three missionary journeys, setting up churches, and writing fourteen epistles. In closing, consider Saul's dying to self and life as a disciple as you read the last scripture: Jesus' call to make disciples.

Belief and Prayer Journal: Is Jesus first in your life? Prayerfully journal as you evaluate each of your interpersonal relationships to make certain that the name of Jesus would not be offensive in any of them. When you spend time with the Lord as a disciple, are you asking the right questions?

DISCIPLESHIP AND BELONGING
TO GOD

Whoever belongs to God hears what God says.
(John 8:47)

Scripture reading:
Genesis 2; John 8:31–47; John 10:24–30
(While reading, watch for anything God is revealing, and record God's revelations and your response in your belief journal.)

Have you ever heard the expression membership has its privileges? Now, some may remember the expression being used as part of an advertising campaign for a major credit card institution. The promotional idea was that, if you met their stringent conditions, you could belong financially to something larger than yourself. To those privileged to qualify, membership came with rewards and status as well as the financial backing of the institution. Just the sight of your name on their plastic card projected the image that you belong. This week we are looking at what the Bible says we should believe about discipleship. Today we center on discipleship as belonging to God with all the Kingdom's privileges.

Let's begin with the need to belong. A quick read of Genesis 2 will unfold how God created mankind in relational hierarchy with the need to belong, first to Himself and second to each other as couples in God's covenant of marriage. If you were to read on in Genesis, you would learn that mankind disobeys God (the fall and sin). The fall distorts this harmonious relational hierarchy by putting enmity between God and humanity. From there, the balance of Scripture simply becomes God revealing and working out His plan to reconcile mankind back into a loving relationship of salvation and belonging through His Son and the Church as the body of Christ. At this point, ask yourself what qualifiers you put on discipleship. Do you consider discipleship and belonging to God as an option, a free choice, a mandate, a responsibility, or a gifted privilege bestowed through Christ?

Now turn to our readings in John. In this first reading, Jesus teaches believers three truths concerning discipleship and belonging. First is permanency of Truth: if believers hold to and practice Jesus' teaching, we will be free in Christ and belong to the family of God through His Sonship forever. Second, there is only a choice between two options: either one is a slave to sin and its father the Devil, or they make a decision to believe the truth and belong to God through a saving relationship in Jesus. Jesus' third teaching involves a simple test of discipleship—those belonging to God hear what God says. This leaves the believer with the idea of hearing the voice of God as the cornerstone of belonging and the hallmark of Christian discipleship. Now as simple as this test is, it has the potential to make some believers anxious due to two common issues. Either they have expectation of an external audible voice in lieu of the Holy Spirit's internal counsel, or they experience difficulty recognizing His voice. Both point to issues in believing the Truth revealed in Scripture. Now, if the test makes you anxious, go back and review Week 4 on beliefs concerning the Holy Spirit and Week 6 on beliefs concerning the Scriptures to help overcome doubt. Keep in mind that it is less important how God speaks to us and more important what we do with what He says. What is important is that He speaks most clearly through His Word. The more we read and learn it, the more we will recognize His voice when He speaks, and the more we will obey and experience a sense of belonging. We end with Jesus as our Shepherd and we His sheep. Sheep are notoriously skittish and docile, requiring guidance and protection from a shepherd. This fact affords this relationship great fodder for Jesus' parables. In ending, as sheep do you know the Shepherd, and are you listening and following His lead? The sense of belonging to God as our Shepherd is both a powerful and an empowering emotion.

Belief and Prayer Journal: Have you considered the privilege of being Christ's disciple not in a prideful way but in the experience of belonging to a God whose saving love is the key to life itself? Pray and meditate on Psalm 23. What Kingdom privileges come through Christ? Does your list include intimacy of relationship, security of Heavenly citizenship, authority of Sonship, assurances of the Holy Spirit, belonging to God, eternal family inheritance, and freedom?

DISCIPLESHIP AND PRAYER

**Lord, teach us to pray, just as John taught his disciples.
(Luke 11:1)**

Scripture reading:
Luke 11:1–13; Matthew 6:1–24; John 14:1–27; Mark 11:12–25;
Matthew 18:15–20
(While reading, watch for anything God is revealing, and record God's
revelations and your response in your belief journal.)

Are you familiar with the idiom "just paying lip service"? Maybe
you know it better as "talking the talk without walking the walk."
It is an idiom which one could apply to the religious leaders of Jesus'
day. You see, the rabbis were famous for adding religious rules to God's
Law (Torah) for things such as worship, prayer, keeping Sabbath, clean
and unclean, and the treatment of neighbor that were often if anything
unpractical to keep. Jesus himself chastised them for bundling huge

burdens on the people without lifting a finger to help (Luke 11:46). When it came to prayer, the Torah commanded the people to daily pray the "Shema" as well as teach it to their children (Deut. 6). "Shema" is a structured prayer that centers on the oneness of God and how God required a person's complete love, devotion, and worship. If that was not difficult enough, God also required them to love their neighbor as themself (Matt. 22:35). In Judaism these are the two great commandments, and it is within this context that the disciples took note of the experiential prayer life of Jesus, so much so that our first reading tells us that while Jesus was praying, one of His disciples made the request, "Lord teach us to pray." In response to that request, Jesus teaches them the Lord's Prayer.

This is not the first time Jesus has taught this prayer. In our second reading, Matthew includes the Lord's Prayer as part of Jesus' teaching on Beatitudes from the Sermon on the Mount. As you read this prayer, take note of the structure compared to the "Shema." The first thing Jesus does is personalize God as "Our Father in heaven." He then structures six petitions: maintaining the Holiness of God, the establishment of His Kingdom, the establishment of His will on earth, providing for our daily needs, forgiveness of sin, and the deliverance from testing and the evil one. Although the church likes to add the doxology Thine is the kingdom, power, and glory forever, Jesus' structure was open-ended teaching. His intent was to provide the disciples with a dynamic prayer model structure that invited them to include personal specific petitions and confessions. Before leaving these two readings, take note of a few things. First, Jesus' teaching on prayer is never isolated. It is most always embedded within parables to aid the disciples' understanding of the deep intimacy of a personal relationship with a loving and caring Father. Second, prayer should never be hypocritical, but private, where there is as much listening to God as petitioning Him. Finally, prayer is an integral part of the disciples' spiritual development by their pursuit of righteousness through disciplines like fasting, silence, solitude, confession, and the study of Scripture.

This brings us to Jesus' teachings on the spiritual nature of prayer and our next reading in John concerning the Holy Spirit as the believer's counselor. Jesus knew that through His death, resurrection, and ascension, His relationship to the disciples was about to change from the physical to that of the spiritual through the Holy Spirit. Prayer as the disciple's pathway to God was also about to take on a new sense of power and authority as they would carry on Jesus' work in the world. They would do even greater work in the world because Jesus was going back to the Father, and now they were to ask of God in the authority and the name of His son Jesus (John 14:12-14). From here, we move on to our reading in Mark where Jesus cleanses the temple and curses the fig tree. In this reading Jesus is providing exemplary evidence of the power of faith and forgiveness, as well as the importance of believing in the outcome of prayer. In our final reading, Jesus teaches on the corporate nature of prayer as a means of forgiveness and mercy.

Belief and Prayer Journal: Do personal and corporate mercy and forgiveness dominate your prayer life? Have you ever added to and used the Lord's Prayer as a model prayer?

DISCIPLESHIP: THE WALK OF THE CROSS AS "DYING TO SELF"

For whoever wants to save his life will lose it, but whoever loses his life for me (Jesus) and the gospel will save it.
(Mark 8:35)

As you read, note how each of the four Gospel readings builds on Jesus' teaching, providing some additional facts helping the reader with their understanding.

Scripture reading: Mark 8:31–38; Matthew 16:21–28; Luke 14:25–34; John 12:23–28; Ephesians 4:17–32
(While reading, watch for anything God is revealing, and record God's revelations and your response in your belief journal.)

D oes the Bible's use of riddles such as the one above intrigue you? Does the Spirit draw your curiosity inward to a search for the author's deeper hidden truth contained within the riddle? In reality, that is the very idea behind the use of a riddle. By definition, a riddle is designed to bend, twist, or tie up the teaching in such a way to produce a hard question, all the while hinting there is a mysterious key to a deeper meaning. For this reason, many teaching sages including Jesus employed riddles in their teaching parables. With this in mind, we turn to today's opening verse, where Jesus teaches: "Whoever loses his life for me and the gospel will save it."

The first twist occurs with the fact that in Greek, the word for life and soul is the same, leaving one to ponder whether Jesus is referring to the physical life or the eternal. The next twist is the process of discipleship which requires the *daily* dying to self, the taking up of one's cross, and the following of Jesus. It is a twist because we consider a well-developed self (self-concept and esteem) of high value. Yet, the scriptures painfully tell us there is no measure to compare the value of the self and its pleasures in this sinful world against the loss of the soul and the glory of eternal life with the Father. The final twist stems from Jesus' expectations of discipleship. In Luke we learn by hyperbole (hating of father, mother, etc.) that we must love Jesus more than our immediate family. Luke also through the parables of "building a tower" and "a king that is evaluating his military strength" teaches that Jesus does not expect blind, naïve commitments. Jesus expects disciples to consider the cost prior to complete surrender.

Jesus' teaching on discipleship as the process of dying to self reached its pinnacle during Passion Week as He exemplified it by completing the Father's will through His walk of the cross. For the Christian disciple, the process of dying to self carries a similar price over the loss of the self and should be grieved as any loss. To aid our understanding on how we are to deal with this grieving process, we turn to a popular grief model developed by Elizabeth Kübler-Ross. In her book *On Death and Dying*, she outlines the five stages of grief that terminally ill and dying patients experience over loss of self: denial, anger, bargaining, depression, and acceptance. As one faces Jesus' requirement to die to self, they also should expect to move through these five stages. The first is denial. Most of us recognize denial as a defense to fend off anxiety. In this process denial will inhibit one from even considering the truth of Jesus' teachings. Once past denial, there is anger which is the emotion expressed by humans when we don't get what we want. Out of this anger stage, we begin the next stage of bargaining. This could be called the "iffy" stage of faith in that our prayers start with "if you do this God" and end with "then I'll do your bidding." Bargaining is our human attempt to retain part of the self. From here we move to stage four: depression. At this point the worldly view of helplessness and hopelessness needs to be replaced with beliefs concerning the biblical truth of the Gospel of Christ as our hope and the Spirit as our help. At the end of the grieving process are acceptance and discipleship. In our last reading, Paul describes this process as having a new attitude where you have put off the old self and put on the new self, created to be like Jesus.

Belief and Prayer Journal: Laying theses stages over your faith walk of discipleship, which stage dominates your walk? When reading Ephesians, does the Spirit reveal any behaviors or beliefs that are holding you in check? Pray for the Spirit's help to fully move to the acceptance stage of discipleship.

DISCIPLESHIP AND THE MINISTRY OF RECONCILIATION

We are therefore Christ's ambassadors, as though God were making his appeal through us. We implore you on Christ's behalf: Be reconciled to God.
(2 Corinthians 5:20)

Scripture reading:
Ephesians 2:14–17; Romans 5:10–11; Colossians 1:15–23;
2 Corinthians 5:1-21
(While reading, watch for anything God is revealing, and record God's revelations and your response in your belief journal.)

As a believer, how do you respond when you have been wronged by another? Do you forgive and work toward reconciling the relationship? How about if you are the guilty party? Do you repent and seek forgiveness while working at reconciling the relationship? Today we are looking at the *ministry of reconciliation* as a fundamental part of the disciple's call to share the good news of Christ, who reconciled believers back to God. Let's begin with defining reconciliation. Reconciliation is the restoring of friendly relations from the enmity and estrangement that was caused to exist between the parties. Now, from the time of Adam and Eve, the sin of disobedience and self-centeredness made us enemies of God. That same sinfulness also introduces strife and enmity into all levels of human relationship making it difficult to love God, let alone your neighbor as yourself. Enmity is the emotional experience of anger, hatred, or hostility stemming from being wronged by another and is directed at the other. It destroys relationships with a mixture of feelings and thoughts concerning disloyalty and disappointment as it shatters one's trust, hopes, and expectations. The more emotionally close in intimacy the other is to us, the more profound and intense the experience as it violates one's confidence in both the other and the relationship itself. Our readings today deal with the two fundamental relationships that the Bible teaches need to be reconciled: *man to his fellow man* and *man to God*.

In the case of *man to his fellow man*, we turn to the scripture readings from Ephesians and Romans where we learn that all believers are equal in God's sight because of Christ's atoning work on the cross and the work of the Spirit. There is no more Jew or Gentile (racism), sexism, or ageism because all believers receive the Spirit. In rebirth the Spirit fundamentally changes all believers, thus beginning the process of regenerating them back to the image of God. The Spirit's process enables *both* parties to change, compromise, forgive and reconcile in God's sight as they resume fellowship.

In the case of *man to God*, our reading in Colossians teaches that the shed blood of Christ puts into effect God's plan of salvation. Through Christ God breaks down man's hostility as the Spirit convinces the believer of the enormity of their sin in the face of God's holiness. God's plan of salvation is a movement of God toward mankind, but mankind has the obligation to accept God's invitation to renounce sin and turn to God in faith and obedience. Once a believer allows the Spirit to make the required changes (imputing Christ's righteousness and atonement), their hostility has been removed so that God can now receive them into a fellowship of love and grace. God's movement to man does not constitute a change in God. Scriptures are clear—God is immutable, which means He never changes (James 1:17). Therefore Paul teaches the church at Corinth in our opening reading that reconciliation is not God to man but man to God and it is possible because a believer is now a new creation in Christ Jesus.

That brings us full circle back to Paul's opening analogy of disciples as ambassadors of Christ the King carrying God's message of peace. Paul is making Christ's message personal, challenging disciples to deliver the call "be reconciled to God" as if Jesus Himself were doing it through you.

Belief and Prayer Journal: As a believer, do you see Paul's challenge as an extension of Jesus' Great Commission (Matthew 28:16-20)? In the Beatitudes Jesus taught that disciples should settle matters of broken relationships quickly especially when it is brother needing reconciled to brother (Matthew 5:24-26). Will the ministry of reconciliation be at the heart of your Easter celebration tomorrow?

Have a blessed Easter.

CPSIA information can be obtained
at www.ICGtesting.com
Printed in the USA
LVHW012302091219
639936LV00014B/426/P